THE POEMS
OF
ERNEST DOWSON

ERNEST DOWSON AT OXFORD

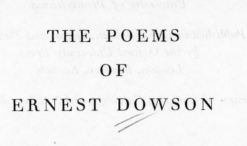

THE POEMS
OF
ERNEST DOWSON

Edited by

Mark Longaker

Philadelphia
University of Pennsylvania Press

7331
Printed in Great Britain by
W. & J. Mackay & Co Ltd, Chatham

46208

EDITOR'S NOTE

The abiding interest in Ernest Dowson and the difficulty in obtaining his poetry are the justification for the present volume. It is the hope of the editor that the introduction and the notes will be helpful to the reader.

M. L.

CONTENTS

CONTENTS

DECORATIONS: IN VERSE AND PROSE (1899)

IN VERSE:

CONTENTS

CONTENTS

ILLUSTRATIONS

INTRODUCTION

ALTHOUGH by no means a poet of the front rank, Ernest Dowson's place in literature is secure. No anthologist who presumes to select the best poems in the language can possibly ignore him, and no literary historian who is concerned with true poetic values can merely identify him with a movement and pass on. That his verse profits by selection cannot be gainsaid, but there is more lyric beauty in his slender volumes than is generally believed. He is far more than a one-poem poet: exquisite as the "Non Sum Qualis Eram Bonae Sub Regno Cynarae" is, it is by no means all of Dowson. One who confines his reading of the poet to "Cynara" misses much that is representative and beautiful.

Nor is the view of the vexed and torn spirit, the refugee in cabmen's shelters, East End dives, and the dimly lighted cafés around Les Halles a complete and balanced portrait of Dowson. It is true that his life was lived among shadows rather than light, but on occasion sunbeams filtered through the wall of cloud with which his heredity and environment surrounded him. His life and character cannot be called exemplary, but it can readily be shown that he was far from the wastrel that he is often pictured. Without laboring the point, one who has familiarized himself with the facts can readily conclude that Dowson was more a victim of circumstance than one who deliberately cultivated life-weariness and chose the path which led to evil and destruction. Of admiration for his life and character there can be little; but it is easy to like Ernest Dowson, and to wish that something might have been done to give him sanctuary from the world and from himself.

Ernest Christopher Dowson was born in Lee in Kent on August 2, 1867, with only a fighting chance for happiness and success. Heredity and the environment of his home played a more important part in his life than is commonly supposed. When in his Introduction to the first collected edition of Dowson's *Poems* (1905) Arthur Symons stated: "Dowson was precisely one of those who owed least to circumstances; and in succumbing to them, he did no more than succumb to destructive forces which, shut up within him, pulled down the house of life upon his own head," he had not given proper weight to the facts. And when, following Symons, Agnes Rothery observed: "While he succeeded in being very completely and very consistently miserable during the thirty-three years of his life, this misery was in no way caused by impaired circumstances of birth and fortune,"[1] she was plainly ill-informed. Surely much of the tragedy of Dowson's life and early death can be traced to his birthright and to the circumstances which surrounded his youth. Although no one will be sufficiently uncharitable to his parents to suggest that they were entirely to blame for his sad life and early death—for they, too, were victims of circumstances over which they had small control—the fact remains that Ernest Dowson had a

[1] "Mad Poets in Spring," *Virginia Quarterly Review*, April, 1927.

poor start. In his birthright there were a few advantages, to be sure; but the disadvantages outweighed them a hundredfold. Others have encountered such disadvantages and overcome them, but their number is few. They are the conquerors among men, to whom there has been given strength—we know not how—to ride out the storm. Dowson was not one of these.

Alfred Dowson, the poet's father, was a man of literary interests and refined tastes, whose small income was derived from Bridge Dock, a drydock on the Thames between Poplar and the Tower which had been in the family for several generations and which in 1867 already showed signs of imminent dissolution. His feeling of economic insecurity heightened a tendency toward hypochondria and gave his frail body little opportunity to combat an inherited predisposition to tuberculosis, which, by the time Ernest was in his early teens, was far advanced. The mother, whose maiden name was Swan, was similarly afflicted. She was a quiet woman who impressed visitors by her gentle manner and her apparent preoccupation with matters hardly cheerful. The frequent trips during the winter to Mentone and Bordighera, on which Ernest was taken along and on which he gained an early fluency in French, did little to check the progression of their disease, nor did these sojourns give them more than a temporary sense of well-being. Emotionally unstable, tuberculous, and increasingly concerned over his dwindling income from the dock, both of them committed suicide within a few months of each other in 1894, when still comparatively young. It is not to be assumed that his parents' troubles were regularly impressed upon the consciousness of the sensitive boy, for the Dowsons were not the sort of parents who take dreams away from their children in order to support their own self-pity; but the fact remains that the atmosphere of his home could do little save direct the inclination toward life-weariness which he expressed before he was out of his teens.

Until he matriculated at Queen's College, Oxford, in 1886, at the age of nineteen, he had had no systematic or formal education. His parents' sojourns in the south of France, and their constant moving from one home to another after 1880, afforded the boy little opportunity to get his roots firmly planted in any one soil, to make and keep friends, and to pursue a well-ordered education. His father, widely read but only sporadically concerned with the boy's training, employed tutors for him in France, and undertook as best he could to supervise and stimulate his reading; but by the time the boy went up to Oxford, he had no particular objective, his background was full of unaccountable gaps, and he had little discipline. W. R. Thomas, one of his acquaintances at Oxford, reported that "Dowson never would have gone up had he been forced to take matrics."[1] His uncle, Alexander Swan, advanced 20 pounds to help meet matriculation expenses. Dowson remained for five terms at Queen's, rooming for the greater part of the time in Number 5 of the attic of the Back Quad, overlooking the cemetery of St. Peter's in the east. After some of the strangeness of university life had worn off, he seemed

[1] "Ernest Dowson at Oxford," *The Nineteenth Century*, April, 1928.

eager to adapt himself to the Oxford pattern. Associating with young men who shared some of his interests led him in time to try to share some of theirs. W. R. Thomas; Arthur Moore, with whom he was to collaborate on two novels, *A Comedy of Masks* (1893) and *Adrian Rome* (1899); Sam Smith, who remained a lifelong friend and correspondent; and Lionel Johnson, with whom he was to associate at the Rhymers' Club and the gatherings at the Crown, were friends who exercised a considerable influence on him at Oxford and in whose company some of his feeling of maladjustment eased. Although the University was unsuccessful in its passive efforts to make of him a well-informed and disciplined man, it augmented interests which he had cultivated in adolescence, especially his reading in the Roman poets Horace, Catullus, and Propertius; in the French poets Baudelaire and Verlaine, who had recently become a topic of lively interest among the *avant-garde* element at Oxford; and in a miscellaneous assortment of English and American authors, of whom John Webster, De Quincey, Swinburne, Poe, and Henry James were his favorites. It was his friendships with such men as Moore and Johnson, as well as the Oxford air, which encouraged him to write stories and poems, some of which were submitted to periodicals and accepted for publication. Suddenly and without plausible explanations to his friends, Dowson left Oxford in March, 1888, after failing to report for his examinations. "I am not for 'Mods' nor 'Mods' for me," he told Thomas upon his departure.[1]

[1] *Ibid.*

His decision to leave Oxford was probably in part dependent on his feeling that he could be of some service to his father at the dock, the affairs of which were in sore need of attention. Down in London, he tried earnestly for a time to fill the role of secretary-book-keeper in the family enterprise, but it was a feeling of obligation rather than any interest in such work which kept him at the ledgers, with increasing irregularity, for over five years. He could scarcely wait to finish adding up the small sums for minor ship repairs so that he might leave for the West End, where he could talk to other young men just down from college about recent French poetry, the "Daycadongs," and his own literary projects. At such then-celebrated gathering places as the Crown, he met and talked with men who were contributing to the tone of the Mauve Decade—Herbert Horne and Selwyn Image, Beardsley, Symons, Le Gallienne, Rhys, John Lane and Elkin Mathews; and on occasion Wilde, fresh from his successes with his plays and poems, and Yeats, full of the insight recently brought to him at Madame Blavatsky's. The spirit of a multifarious renaissance was in those gatherings, and Dowson was aware of its pulse. With such stimulating company and with an increasing awareness of his talents, he began to contribute poems and stories to such well-established periodicals as the *Century Guild Hobby Horse* and the *Yellow Book*. The years between his leaving Oxford and the time of the death of his parents in 1894 were his most productive. Most of the poems which were to be included in *Verses* (1896) and *Decorations: In Verse and Prose* (1899) were written in this interval, as were his verse play *The*

Pierrot of the Minute (unpublished until 1897), the two novels with Arthur Moore, most of the stories which he included in *Dilemmas* (1895), and a large number of translations from the French, including Zola's *La Terre* (1894). These were Dowson's happiest years. Gatherings at the Crown, Thursday nights at the Rhymers' Club, plays and meetings with Bensonian actors such as Marmaduke Langdale and Lennox Pawle, commendation of his talent on all sides. And in spite of sinister signs that all was not well at home and with his own health, he could dismiss them in the glow of satisfaction which came with the recognition of his art.

In the early nineties Dowson lived in a climate well removed from the dimly lighted cafés of the East End and the alleylike tributaries off the boulevard St. Michel. The portrait of the poet of the cabmen's shelters and East End dives needs modification if not complete revision, for at this time Dowson was even in danger of becoming what Plarr called "a fashionable poet." Although by no means a brilliant *diseur*, he carried on, with men and women known for their erudition and wit, conversations entirely in keeping with his increasingly wide reputation as a poet, and his manner was not without charm. His garb was becoming to the company he kept: his suits bore the label of a good London tailor, his boots were made on lasts designed by a bootmaker who catered to the fashionable trade, and his hats rivaled those of the dandies who were seen regularly in the circle of the Alhambra and at the Café Royal. When Horace Vachell told Gertrude Atherton in 1896, "It must be years since he has spoken to a decent woman—if he ever knew one,"[1] he left a totally false impression. The "Dowson legend" thus perpetuated can be modified if not rejected altogether by recalling that during the first half of the nineties the poet attended the *salons* of Sir John and Lady Simon of Kensington Square and Sir Joseph and Lady Prestwich, besides knowing the charming old lady who spoke about "the young Mr. Gladstone," such talented and decorative ladies as Miss Ida North, Miss Olive Curtois, Mrs. Warr, and a dozen and more women who were carrying on the tradition of Mrs. Thrale. "I know a heap of persons," he wrote to Edgar Jepson in 1895, "and get as many cards for private showings as if I were a celebrity."[2]

It was sometime in 1891 that he met "Missie," Adelaide Foltinowicz, with whom he fell in love. She was the great passion of his life, and it was to her that he dedicated his poems in *Verses* (1896). She was a vivacious twelve-year-old when he saw her first in her father's restaurant at 19 Sherwood Street, a cheap but entirely respectable eating place to which Dowson and his friends Moore, Langdale, and Jepson went for supper, sometimes as often as four times a week. Although to many of the poet's friends it seemed unusual that a talented young man just down from college who had the qualifications for becoming a fashionable poet should waste his time and affection on the uncomprehending daughter of a Polish immigrant, the attachment was by no means

[1] Gertrude Atherton, *Adventures of a Novelist* (London, 1932), p. 109.
[2] Mark Longaker, *Ernest Dowson* (Philadelphia, 1945), 2nd ed., p. 195.

unique, nor was there anything in it to suggest abnormality or depravity. Fondness, even abiding love, for little girls had its precedents among men of letters and elsewhere; and although such attachments are unusual, there need not be anything sinister in them. Dowson loved her for her innocence, in which he found a sort of sanctifying grace. His own physical weakness, of which he was only dimly aware, and the restrained and sombre mood of his life at home intensified his enjoyment of the girl's animated prattle; and in her vitality and youth he found much that was both appealing and strengthening. Nor was the relationship between Dowson and Adelaide the "exquisite impossibility" which Arthur Symons and others felt they detected. Although he recognized the inevitability of her growing into womanhood, he seriously planned to marry her when she was of age. Neither Adelaide nor her parents were opposed to the prospect; and in spite of the fact that the Foltinowiczes no doubt were flattered by the attentions which Dowson paid their daughter and his expressed intent to marry her when she came of age, they did nothing to hasten the day, nor was there any attempt to ensnare him. It is a mistaken notion that has become part of the "Dowson legend" that Adelaide led him on and then cast him out. The unsuitability of the union became more and more obvious to both the parents and Adelaide, if not to Dowson; and when in September, 1897, she married Auguste, a waiter in the restaurant, a relationship which had run an undulating course for six years was ended. That Dowson's attachment was the inspiration for much of his poetry and the source of much of his distress is plain, but the idea that Adelaide both made and destroyed a poet is not supported by the facts.

The tragic circumstances surrounding the death of both his parents in the fall of 1894 were probably the turning point of the poet's life. "I always thought," said Robert Sherard to the present editor, "that it was his mother's death, following so closely upon his father's, which jostled his little ambition to live and create over the borderline."[1] There is no doubt that after his mother's death Dowson was a changed man. Without compelling ambition, without strength of either body or spirit, and now without the fragile ties of family and home, he took—or rather, he was forced to take—the road which led down instead of up.

There was a long period of emptiness in his life following his mother's death. Ill-health, indecision, and life-sickness all contributed to the void which surrounded him. His younger brother Rowland, with whom he had never been companionable, went to live with relatives for a time before going to Canada.[2] It was suggested that Ernest accompany his brother, a prospect in which he showed no interest. The house in Kent was given up, and for a time he lived in the dilapidated house which was part of Bridge Dock, the income from which by this time was almost negligible. The atmosphere of the place was depressing to both his body and spirit, but it was not until the summer of 1895 that his slight instinct toward

---

[1] *Op. cit.*, p. 165.

[2] After a short time in Canada, where he found the life strenuous and the climate inhospitable to his diseased lungs, Rowland moved to San Diego, California, where he died shortly after the turn of the century.

self-preservation led him to pack his slender wardrobe, a bundle of manuscripts including his "Poesie Schublade," a few books, most of which belonged to friends, and take a room in Bloomsbury, from where he made a half-hearted effort to pick up his former interests.

Despite the fact that Bloomsbury was near the center of things and that a few of his friends tried to help him make out a plan for his immediate future, he left London for France in the late summer of 1895, and after staying for a while in Dieppe, went on to Paris. From this time, save for a few increasingly brief intervals, Dowson's movements are indistinct: 214, rue St. Jacques, Paris, during the winter of 1895–1896; the Hôtel Gloanec, Pont-Aven, which he called "for a time at least my permanent home and address"; back in London in the summer of 1896 to look after assignments in translating for Smithers, to arrange for the publication of his first volume of poems, *Verses*, and to collect the pittance which had accumulated at Bridge Dock; a trip to Ireland where he apparently visited friends and from where he gave the address "c/o I. De Courcy Macdonell, Esq., Fairy Hill, Limerick, Ireland"; back in Paris in the winter of 1896–1897 at the Hôtel Odessa, and again in Brittany in the spring and summer. He planned a long sojourn on the Riviera and Italy with the painter Loiseau for the winter of 1897, but this, like his plans to go to Algiers to see "les jolies femmes arabesques," and to visit with Oscar Wilde in Naples, was never carried out. On increasingly rare occasions he turned up in London, to say of his brief visits to Plarr: "I hate it, when I am here; and go away anywhere, thankfully;

but alas! such is my inconsistency, that when I have been but a little while from it, as says Johnson, that great lexicographer whom you blaspheme, 'I take the first convenient opportunity of returning to a place, where, if there is not much happiness, there is, at least such a diversity of good and evil, that slight vexations do not fix upon the heart.' " Back and forth from London to Paris to Pont-Aven in 1898 and until the fall of 1899, translating erotica for Smithers at thirty shillings a week, and getting together verses for his second volume *Decorations: In Verse and Prose* (1899), never staying at any one place for more than a few months at a time—"in search of that we know not."

On a Friday in late December, 1899, Robert Sherard found him in a pub on Bedford Street, emaciated and virtually penniless, suffering from what Dowson called "an enfeebling influenza." Sherard, who had known the poet quite intimately in London as early as 1892 and who had helped him only a few months earlier in Paris, saw the seriousness of Dowson's condition. He took him to his home in Catford, where he and his wife looked after him for six weeks. Despite occasional signs of recovery of health and spirits, Dowson died in Sherard's home on February 23, 1900.

There is small doubt that his death at the age of thirty-three was hastened by irregular living and intemperate habits. Modern science would probably name as a contributing factor the excessive use of alcohol, especially absinthe, which is regarded by some as extremely destructive to body and mind. To one who has familiarized himself with the facts, however, this side of the poet's

nature has been exaggerated, and some of its manifesta-
tions have been invented. A well-informed and charitable
view can trace Dowson's early death to a combination of
destructive forces, the complexity of which most of his
commentators have chosen to simplify to his disservice.
Louis Untermeyer in the biographical note to the
selection of Dowson poems for his *Modern British Poetry*
(1920) stated: "For almost two years he lived in sordid
supper-houses known as 'cabmen's shelters'. . . . He
literally drank himself to death." And even Yeats, in
his B.B.C. talk on the Rhymers' Club, after admitting
that he envied Dowson his "dissipated life", gave
momentum to the legend by stating: "Years were to
pass before I discovered that Dowson's life, except when
he came to the Rhymers', or called upon some friend
selected for an extreme respectability, was a sordid round
of drink and cheap harlots."[1]

In order to make the picture of desolation more
complete, many of his commentators have made him out
to be not only a drunkard but a drug addict as well. In
the Introduction to his edition of Dowson's poems, Arthur
Symons, after stating that "without a certain sordidness
in his surroundings he was never quite comfortable,
never quite himself," reported: "At Oxford, I believe,
his favourite form of intoxication had been haschisch
. . .," and Francis Gribble, confessing that his remark
was drawn from hearsay, stated: ". . . . hashish, they
say, was Dowson's most formidable enemy."[2] Such
reports are entirely inaccurate. Edgar Jepson, Conal

[1] *The Listener*, October 14, 1936.
[2] *Seen in Passing*, London, 1929.

O'Riordan, Robert Sherard, and Arthur Moore, among others who knew Dowson intimately, are as one in reporting that these stories about the poet's addiction to drugs are unattested rumors which probably had their origin in a few harmless undergraduate experiments. And as for his excessive drinking "the poisonous liquors of those pothouses which swarm about the docks," there were many long intervals—not only the six weeks before his death in Sherard's home—when he "literally" drank nothing stronger than the Brittany cider which was included in the *pension* at the Hôtel Gloanec. Oversimplification and a sense of the theatrical were responsible for the origin and perpetuation of the Dowson legend, which was created almost entirely by men who knew him only slightly, or not at all. *Tout comprendre, c'est tout pardonner*.

The Dowson legend fortunately has done the poet slight disservice. It is a sad commentary on human nature that some poets have at times gained a part of their audience on account of the evil attributed to their lines and lives. Dowson is no exception. There is no doubt, however, that his readers, no matter what the ultimate source of their interest in his poetry has been, have found a consummate artistry that makes any biographical reference secondary. Dowson was weak in both body and will; he aggravated the weaknesses which were thrust upon him by birth and training by irregularities in living which were in some measure of his own devising. But out of the bludgeonings of circumstance which have left other men mumbling incoherent blasphemies, he fashioned a dark beauty which leaves few unmoved.

Virtually all of Dowson's poetry was printed in his lifetime in two slender volumes, *Verses* (1896) and *Decorations: In Verse and Prose* (1899). The verse play *The Pierrot of the Minute*, written in 1892, was not published until 1897; and the poems which he had written out in his "Poesie Schublade," which he rejected for inclusion in *Verses* and *Decorations*, were not printed until 1934, at which time Desmond Flower in his edition of *The Poetical Works of Ernest Christopher Dowson* included them in the "Hitherto Unpublished Poems" section. Two poems which appeared after the poet's death which he had not included in his two volumes were printed in periodicals from manuscripts he had sent to friends.[1] Manuscript versions of some of the poems in *Verses* and *Decorations* continue to show up, but it is unlikely that any significant body of Dowson's work remains undiscovered.[2]

Although there is little latitude and variety in Dowson's poetry, it lends itself to useful classification. Allowing for a frequent overlapping of theme and mood, the reader finds poems which deal with nature and with love, some devotional poetry, a few occasional poems addressed

[1] The friends to whom these poems were sent cannot be determined. One of the poems, "The Passing of Tennyson," was printed by Holbrook Jackson in *T. P.'s Weekly* early in 1915; the other, "Fantasie Triste," appeared in *Known Signatures* as late as 1932 and was drawn from item Number 206 in the Elkin Matthews–A. J. A. Symons catalogue.

[2] The Dowson items that were in the House of Smithers at the time of its dissolution are probably irretrievably lost. Most of these items, however, were translations from the French, with possibly a few tales which had not been taken by the *Savoy*. In the light of persuasive evidence, it can be concluded that there were few if any poems, for Dowson wrote little poetry after 1897.

to particular friends in connection with special events, and a considerable number of poems which reveal a recurrent if not an abiding life-weariness. Shifting the plan of classification from the thematic to the formal, one finds in addition to the poems grouped topically which are all lyrical, the dramatic narrative verse-play *The Pierrot of the Minute* and the five prose poems in *Decorations*.

The label "nature poems" must be promptly qualified if it is to be used in referring to a considerable number of the poems, for the element of nature is generally employed in order to establish the emotional background and set the mood rather than to disclose an attitude towards nature or to express a philosophy. In spite of the explicit lines in his sonnet "To Nature":

> Thou unclean harpy, odorous of despair,
> I offer up no praises on the shrine
> Of thy wild beauty; thou art not divine,
> Nor reverent at all thy tranquil air.

the poet had no deliberated conviction that nature was malevolent or even indifferent. What had become a point of anguish for Thomas Hardy in "Nature's Questioning" was well removed from Dowson's way of thinking. It is true that he saw the autumnal rather than the springtime hues of nature: even in the sonnet "My Lady April" he sees the showers as tears, and

> Autumn and withered leaves and vanity,
> And winter bringing end in barrenness.

The tone of these poems, however, is more the reflection of a quality in the poet's nature than the projection of a well-considered conviction. Such poems as the "Villanelle of Sunset," "A Coronal," and "Breton Afternoon," among other poems which can be included in the group, all show the poet responsive to nature's more somber moods, and apparently delighted to linger over the refinements of response which these moods create. It is in his use of nature imagery and in his exploration of sensory and emotional response to autumnal hues that much of the decadent spirit is found.

The label "love poems," too, must be promptly qualified, for Dowson was a love poet in a distinctive if not an entirely unique way. Although there are occasional tributes to the delights of wanton love as in the rondeau "Ah, Manon, say, why is it we," and an infrequent Herrick-like theme and mood of "Gather ye rosebuds while ye may" cast into a blithe Cavalier measure, the recurrent theme grows out of the poignancy of unrequited love and especially the love that fails in fulfillment because it seeks an abiding virginal innocence. Many of his love poems are versified expressions of his recognition of the inevitability of the changes that attend growth. "What a terrible, lamentable thing growth is!" he exclaimed in a letter to his friend Victor Plarr. "Ad Domnulam Suam," "Yvonne of Brittany," "In Tempore Senectutis," and the justly famous "Cynara" show this distinctive theme projected through varying moods. Although these poems are clearly in keeping with the decadent spirit of the nineties, especially in their diction and their obvious though unobtrusive manipulation of tonal effects, they cannot be considered only as consummate examples of the application of the principles of the decadent aesthetic, much less dismissed as rhetoric. These poems grew out of heightened emotional experience integrated into flawless artistic achievements. The trade of writing this kind of poetry is a dangerous one: without valid experience or without proper objectification of experience this kind of poetry can descend to the level of Arthur Symons' "Bianca" poems, and his "To One in Alienation," in which the theme of "Cynara" recurs with unfortunate results. The distinctive quality and merit of Dowson's love poetry can be traced to the fact that the life and personality of the poet and the decadent spirit were mutually congenial.

When C. E. Andrews and M. O. Percival in the Introduction to their anthology *Poetry of the Nineties* (1926) observed that Dowson wavered "between heaping garlands upon the altars of Aphrodite and lighting candles to the blessed Virgin," they unintentionally left the impression that Dowson's devotional poetry was of considerable volume. Furthermore, neither phrase is critically sound, for the poet put few garlands on the altar of Aphrodite and lighted even fewer candles to the Virgin. Only four of the poems can be called devotional: "The Nuns of the Perpetual Adoration," "Benedictio Domini," and "Extreme Unction" in *Verses*, and "Carthusians" in *Decorations*. Both internal and external evidence indicate that these poems, despite the differences in time of their initial appearance in print, were written in 1891–1892 during the time preparatory to and immediately following his conversion. This need not imply that he forsook the Church after 1892; rather it suggests that he did not find in religion an abiding source of inspiration for poetry.

Dowson was not a Catholic poet in the sense that Francis Thompson, Coventry Patmore, Alice Meynell, and his friend Lionel Johnson were. There is only one poem, "Extreme Unction," dedicated to Johnson, which can be termed peculiarly Catholic. It is a mistaken notion, however, that Dowson became a Catholic only on account of the pageantry and ritual. Although the beauty of the ritual no doubt played a part in his conversion, as did the sense of tradition and historicity, it is denying Dowson his very considerable intelligence to assume that he based his decision to embrace the Church only on the appeal of ecclesiastical regalia, beautifully wrought censers, and Ave Marias. His conversations with his friends, his annotations of Olive Schreiner's *African Farm*, and his feeling of need for something to which to moor all indicate that his conversion was the result of careful and prayerful deliberation. When Lionel Johnson wrote "The Faun among the Satyrs," he did not have Dowson in mind.

That his conversion promptly proved disappointing is hardly the case. It is true that few devotional poems were written after he went into the Church, and that his sense of good and evil became no more acute. To him, religion and morals had little in common. He made no pretense of leading a consistently devout Catholic life. But all this need not indicate that he found the Church wanting. He probably never expected a sign to be given, or that the heavens would fall. He did not crave mystical revelation and experience. All his poetry stands as proof that Dowson was one of those men who, instead of expecting too much, expect too little. And in his entering the Church he wanted little more than peace. All the devotional poems, with the exception of the last stanza of "Extreme Unction," bear this out.

The occasional poems addressed to particular people in connection with special events are represented by "On the Birth of a Friend's Child" in *Verses*, "To William Theodore Peters on His Renaissance Cloak" in *Decorations*, and "The Passing of Tennyson," which was not printed until 1915 in *T. P.'s Weekly*. These are tasteful, prettily turned eulogies which are scarcely characteristic of the poet's themes or manner. Victor Plarr, to whom the first of these poems was addressed, liked it but at the same time felt that he would have preferred a measure more in keeping with the poet's talent than the neatly turned heroic couplets. It is obvious that Dowson had little interest in occasional poetry.

The life-weariness poems are by far the most numerous. In fact, in most of the poems which deal with nature, love, and religion some of this quality appears. The ennui of these poems is not a French importation save in the Gallic connotations of the word, nor was it the result of the poet's awareness of the time-weariness that attended the closing years of a burdened century. It is true that Dowson was entirely familiar with the suggestions which lie in the French ennui and spleen. He knew the Verlaine poems "C'est l'extase langoureuse" and "Il pleure dans mon coeur" in "Ariettes oubliées" and "Spleen" in "Aquarelles"; he translated these into English verse not as literary exercises but as poems into which he could project much that was singularly his own. Many of the English decadents of the nineties toyed with the theme of ennui—witness Arthur Symons' poem "Satiety"—but this was a French importation which did not transplant well to the banks of the Thames. Dowson, however, had ennui as part of his birthright; and as the years passed, with their accumulation of misfortunes, he experienced an ever increasing sense of weariness. To him it was not a pose or a deliberately cultivated temporary condition out of which a poem might emerge; "the empty longing for a new wish" was a real and frequently recurrent state of mind and spirit which found expression not only in the excellent translations of Verlaine, but in such poems as "To One in Bedlam" and "Spleen" in *Verses*, and "Dregs" and "A Last Word" in *Decorations*.

His one venture into the field of sustained dramatic narrative verse, the play *The Pierrot of the Minute*, was plainly a digression which he undertook at the request of the poet-actor William Theodore Peters. In spite of the fact that he was working in a métier with which he was unfamiliar and for which he professed to have no talent, he finished the play in the prescribed two weeks and was apparently pleased with Peters' production. It is a fragile little piece with the lines cast largely into rhymed couplets, a metrical form which helps to produce some of the effect of an eighteenth-century pastel. The narrative element is slight: the play was written more as an evocation of mood than as a dramatic resolution of conflict.

The prose poems which form the second part of *Decorations* are apparently only experiments in polyphonic prose. In the light of the circumstances surrounding their writing, however, these pieces cannot be dismissed as the work of a theorist seeking a vehicle for experimentation. In all of them, with the exception of the trifle "Markets," the allegory is plain. Dowson was one of the few poets who preferred prose to verse, and in his statement of preference, he recognized the poetic effects which can be attained in prose. "Absinthia Taetra" and "The Visit" illustrate his success in creating poetic effects through visual and tonal imagery in prose.

The texts of the poems in the present volume are those of the original editions, with the exception of a few corrections, chiefly of misprints, by former editors. The original arrangements are preserved. Although some critics feel that the poems in *Verses* constitute a cycle whose unity needs emphasizing, it is difficult to discover any consecutiveness of plan. The poems in both *Verses* and *Decorations* are certainly neither chronologically nor topically arranged. The first poem in *Verses*, "A Coronal," was written two years later than "My Lady April," the fourth poem in the volume; and "The Nuns of the Perpetual Adoration," the second poem in the collection, obviously has no relationship in theme, mood, or structure to either of them. And interestingly enough, the last poem in *Decorations*, "A Last Word," for all of its tone of finality, was written in large part as early as 1886. Although a chronological sequence would be interesting to the biographer who wishes to try to trace the development of a poet's mind and art, in Dowson's case there is little or no critical value in trying to place his poems into particular periods. Virtually all of his poetry was written in an interval of less than ten years, 1888–1896; and during this time the inner forces and external influences which gave direction to his poetry remained essentially the same. There is no early or late Dowson; and although some of his critics detect a perceptible falling off in the quality of his verse after 1894, this deterioration, if it exists, is not always the result of the passage of time. Some of his earliest poems are among his best; and some of his late poems are as good as the best. Although no clear plan, chronological or topical, can be discovered in the poet's arrangement of his verses, even if a satisfactory chronological order could be established, it would be of little critical significance.

In the present volume, the editor has made no attempt to compare in full and precise detail the various versions of the poems as they exist in manuscripts, printings in periodicals, and in the texts of the first and subsequent editions of *Verses* and *Decorations*. So many trifling variations appear in the poems in *Verses* and *Decorations* and their original printings in periodicals and their occasional manuscript versions that an exhaustive collation of texts is neither practicable nor necessary. The differences are largely in punctuation, to which, it might appear, Dowson attached a great deal of importance. In few of these instances does the change affect to any appreciable degree the theme or mood of the poem, or give noticeably different inflection even to the reading of the particular line; nor do the poet's latest revisions for *Verses* and *Decorations* indicate a consistent tendency. In some instances a comma yields to a semicolon; but just as often it is the semicolon that yields. Generally speaking, the latest revisions are to the poem's advantage.

There is no doubt that Dowson was a painstaking crafts-man, that he pondered *le mot juste* at length, and that he attached importance to the arrangement of stanzaic patterns. It is equally true that some of poems which he appended to letters written to friends were punctuated without long deliberation; and that his reading of proof for *The Pierrot of the Minute* and *Decorations* was an ordeal which he had neither the energy nor the inclina-tion to prolong. The eventual conclusion to anyone who has examined the variants is that a variorum Dowson would have little critical utility, and no interest save to a textual statistician. This conclusion is supported by the fact that for a full appreciation of Dowson's kind of poetry it is unnecessary to try to discover qualities and meanings that possibly might be disclosed by slightly variant readings. In instances in which the poet's revisions show significant tendencies, the editor has tried to supply adequate information in the Notes. The Notes were provided, however, not in order to inform the reader of the variants in texts, but rather to place the individual poems into biographical and critical per-spective.

Philadelphia, June, 1962   M. L.

VERSES

Vitae summa brevis spem nos vetat incohare longam.

They are not long, the weeping and the laughter,
    Love and desire and hate:
I think they have no portion in us after
    We pass the gate.

They are not long, the days of wine and roses:
    Out of a misty dream
Our path emerges for a while, then closes
    Within a dream.

IN PREFACE: FOR ADELAIDE

To you, who are my verses, as on some very future day, if you ever care to read them, you will understand, would it not be somewhat trivial to dedicate any one verse, as I may do, in all humility, to my friends? Trivial, too, perhaps, only to name you even here? Trivial, presumptuous? For I need not write your name for you at least to know that this and all my work is made for you in the first place, and I need not to be reminded by my critics that I have no silver tongue such as were fit to praise you. So for once you shall go indedicate, if not quite anonymous; and I will only commend my little book to you in sentences far beyond my poor compass which will help you perhaps to be kind to it:

'*Votre personne, vos moindres mouvements me semblaient avoir dans le monde une importance extrahumaine. Mon cœur comme de la poussière se soulevait derrière vos pas. Vous me faisiez l'effet d'un clair-de-lune par une nuit d'été, quand tout est parfums, ombres douces, blancheurs, infini; et les délices de la chair et de l'âme étaient contenues pour moi dans votre nom que je me répétais en tachant de le baiser sur mes lèvres.*

'*Quelquefois vos paroles me reviennent comme un écho lointain, comme le son d'une cloche apporté par le vent; et il me semble que vous êtes là quand je lis des passages de l'amour dans les livres. . . . Tout ce qu'on y blâme d'exagéré, vous me l'avez fait ressentir.*'

PONT-AVEN, FINISTÈRE, 1896.

A CORONAL

With His songs and Her days to His Lady
and to Love

Violets and leaves of vine,
Into a frail, fair wreath
We gather and entwine:
A wreath for Love to wear,
Fragrant as his own breath,
To crown his brow divine,
All day till night is near.
Violets and leaves of vine
We gather and entwine.

Violets and leaves of vine
For Love that lives a day,
We gather and entwine.
All day till Love is dead,
Till eve falls, cold and gray,
These blossoms, yours and mine,
Love wears upon his head.
Violets and leaves of vine
We gather and entwine.

Violets and leaves of vine,
    For Love when poor Love dies
We gather and entwine.
    This wreath that lives a day
    Over his pale, cold eyes,
Kissed shut by Proserpine,
    At set of sun we lay:
Violets and leaves of vine
We gather and entwine.

NUNS OF THE PERPETUAL ADORATION

For THE COUNTESS SOBIESKA VON PLATT

Calm, sad, secure; behind high convent walls,
  These watch the sacred lamp, these watch and pray:
And it is one with them when evening falls,
  And one with them the cold return of day.

These heed not time; their nights and days they make
  Into a long, returning rosary,
Whereon their lives are threaded for Christ's sake:
  Meekness and vigilance and chastity.

A vowed patrol, in silent companies,
  Life-long they keep before the living Christ:
In the dim church, their prayers and penances
  Are fragrant incense to the Sacrificed.

Outside, the world is wild and passionate;
  Man's weary laughter and his sick despair
Entreat at their impenetrable gate:
  They heed no voices in their dream of prayer.

They saw the glory of the world displayed;
  They saw the bitter of it, and the sweet;
They knew the roses of the world should fade,
  And be trod under by the hurrying feet.

Therefore they rather put away desire,
    And crossed their hands and came to sanctuary;
And veiled their heads and put on coarse attire:
    Because their comeliness was vanity.

And there they rest; they have serene insight
    Of the illuminating dawn to be:
Mary's sweet Star dispels for them the night,
    The proper darkness of humanity.

Calm, sad, secure; with faces worn and mild:
    Surely their choice of vigil is the best?
Yea! for our roses fade, the world is wild;
    But there, beside the altar, there, is rest.

VILLANELLE OF SUNSET

Come hither, Child! and rest:
This is the end of day,
Behold the weary West!

Sleep rounds with equal zest
Man's toil and children's play:
Come hither, Child! and rest.

My white bird, seek thy nest,
Thy drooping head down lay:
Behold the weary West!

Now are the flowers confest
Of slumber: sleep, as they!
Come hither, Child! and rest.

Now eve is manifest,
And homeward lies our way:
Behold the weary West!

Tired flower! upon my breast,
I would wear thee alway:
Come hither, Child! and rest;
Behold, the weary West!

MY LADY APRIL

For LÉOPOLD NELKEN

Dew on her robe and on her tangled hair;
Twin dewdrops for her eyes; behold her pass,
With dainty step brushing the young, green grass,
The while she trills some high, fantastic air,
Full of all feathered sweetness: she is fair,
And all her flower-like beauty, as a glass,
Mirrors out hope and love: and still, alas!
Traces of tears her languid lashes wear.

Say, doth she weep for very wantonness?
Or is it that she dimly doth foresee
Across her youth the joys grow less and less,
The burden of the days that are to be:
Autumn and withered leaves and vanity,
And winter bringing end in barrenness.

TO ONE IN BEDLAM

For HENRY DAVRAY

With delicate, mad hands, behind his sordid bars,
Surely he hath his posies, which they tear and twine;
Those scentless wisps of straw, that miserably line
His strait, caged universe, whereat the dull world stares,

Pedant and pitiful. O, how his rapt gaze wars
With their stupidity! Know they what dreams divine
Lift his long, laughing reveries like enchaunted wine,
And make his melancholy germane to the stars'?

O lamentable brother! if those pity thee,
Am I not fain of all thy lone eyes promise me;
Half a fool's kingdom, far from men who sow and reap,
All their days, vanity? Better than mortal flowers,
Thy moon-kissed roses seem: better than love or sleep,
The star-crowned solitude of thine oblivious hours!

AD DOMNULAM SUAM

Little lady of my heart!
    Just a little longer,
Love me: we will pass and part,
    Ere this love grow stronger.

I have loved thee, Child! too well,
    To do aught but leave thee:
Nay! my lips should never tell
    Any tale, to grieve thee.

Little lady of my heart!
    Just a little longer,
I may love thee: we will part,
    Ere my love grow stronger.

Soon thou leavest fairy-land;
    Darker grow thy tresses:
Soon no more of hand in hand;
    Soon no more caresses!

Little lady of my heart!
    Just a little longer,
Be a child: then, we will part,
    Ere this love grow stronger.

AMOR UMBRATILIS

A gift of Silence, sweet!
   Who may not ever hear:
To lay down at your unobservant feet,
   Is all the gift I bear.

I have no songs to sing,
   That you should heed or know:
I have no lilies, in full hands, to fling
   Across the path you go.

I cast my flowers away,
   Blossoms unmeet for you!
The garland I have gathered in my day:
   My rosemary and rue.

I watch you pass and pass,
   Serene and cold: I lay
My lips upon your trodden, daisied grass,
   And turn my life away.

Yea, for I cast you, sweet!
   This one gift, you shall take:
Like ointment, on your unobservant feet,
   My silence, for your sake.

AMOR PROFANUS

For GABRIEL DE LAUTREC

Beyond the pale of memory,
In some mysterious dusky grove;
A place of shadows utterly,
Where never coos the turtle-dove,
A world forgotten of the sun:
I dreamed we met when day was done,
And marvelled at our ancient love.

Met there by chance, long kept apart,
We wandered, through the darkling glades;
And that old language of the heart
We sought to speak: alas! poor shades!
Over our pallid lips had run
The waters of oblivion,
Which crown all loves of men or maids.

In vain we stammered: from afar
Our old desire shone cold and dead:
That time was distant as a star,
When eyes were bright and lips were red.
And still we went with downcast eye
And no delight in being nigh,
Poor shadows most uncomforted.

Ah, Lalage! while life is ours,
Hoard not thy beauty rose and white,
But pluck the pretty, fleeting flowers
That deck our little path of light:
For all too soon we twain shall tread
The bitter pastures of the dead:
Estranged, sad spectres of the night.

VILLANELLE OF MARGUERITES

For MISS EUGÉNIE MAGNUS

'A little, passionately, not at all?'
She casts the snowy petals on the air:
And what care we how many petals fall!

Nay, wherefore seek the seasons to forestall?
It is but playing, and she will not care,
A little, passionately, not at all!

She would not answer us if we should call
Across the years: her visions are too fair;
And what care we how many petals fall!

She knows us not, nor recks if she enthrall
With voice and eyes and fashion of her hair,
A little, passionately, not at all!

Knee-deep she goes in meadow grasses tall,
Kissed by the daisies that her fingers tear:
And what care we how many petals fall!

We pass and go: but she shall not recall
What men we were, nor all she made us bear:
'A little, passionately, not at all!'
And what care we how many petals fall!

YVONNE OF BRITTANY

For MARMADUKE LANGDALE

In your mother's apple-orchard,
　　Just a year ago, last spring:
Do you remember, Yvonne!
　　The dear trees lavishing
Rain of their starry blossoms
　　To make you a coronet?
Do you ever remember, Yvonne?
　　As I remember yet.

In your mother's apple-orchard,
　　When the world was left behind:
You were shy, so shy, Yvonne!
　　But your eyes were calm and kind.
We spoke of the apple harvest,
　　When the cider press is set,
And such-like trifles, Yvonne!
　　That doubtless you forget.

In the still, soft Breton twilight,
　　We were silent; words were few,
Till your mother came out chiding,
　　For the grass was bright with dew:
But I know your heart was beating,
　　Like a fluttered, frightened dove.
Do you ever remember, Yvonne?
　　That first faint flush of love?

In the fulness of midsummer,
  When the apple-bloom was shed,
Oh, brave was your surrender,
  Though shy the words you said.
I was glad, so glad, Yvonne!
  To have led you home at last;
Do you ever remember, Yvonne!
  How swiftly the days passed?

In your mother's apple-orchard
  It is grown too dark to stray,
There is none to chide you, Yvonne!
  You are over far away.
There is dew on your grave grass, Yvonne!
  But your feet it shall not wet:
No, you never remember, Yvonne!
  And I shall soon forget.

BENEDICTIO DOMINI

For SELWYN IMAGE

Without, the sullen noises of the street!
   The voice of London, inarticulate,
Hoarse and blaspheming, surges in to meet
   The silent blessing of the Immaculate.

Dark is the church, and dim the worshippers,
   Hushed with bowed heads as though by some old spell,
While through the incense-laden air there stirs
   The admonition of a silver bell.

Dark is the church, save where the altar stands,
   Dressed like a bride, illustrious with light,
Where one old priest exalts with tremulous hands
   The one true solace of man's fallen plight.

Strange silence here: without, the sounding street
   Heralds the world's swift passage to the fire:
O Benediction, perfect and complete!
   When shall men cease to suffer and desire?

GROWTH

I watched the glory of her childhood change,
Half-sorrowful to find the child I knew,
   (Loved long ago in lily-time)
Become a maid, mysterious and strange,
With fair, pure eyes—dear eyes, but not the eyes I knew
     Of old, in the olden time!

Till on my doubting soul the ancient good
Of her dear childhood in the new disguise
   Dawned, and I hastened to adore
The glory of her waking maidenhood,
And found the old tenderness within her deepening eyes,
     But kinder than before.

AD MANUS PUELLAE

For LEONARD SMITHERS

I was always a lover of ladies' hands!
  Or ever mine heart came here to tryst,
For the sake of your carved white hands' commands;
    The tapering fingers, the dainty wrist;
    The hands of a girl were what I kissed.

I remember an hand like a *fleur-de-lys*
  When it slid from its silken sheath, her glove;
With its odours passing ambergris:
    And that was the empty husk of a love.
    Oh, how shall I kiss your hands enough?

They are pale with the pallor of ivories;
  But they blush to the tips like a curled sea-shell:
What treasure, in kingly treasuries,
    Of gold, and spice for the thurible,
    Is sweet as her hands to hoard and tell?

I know not the way from your finger-tips,
  Nor how I shall gain the higher lands,
The citadel of your sacred lips:
    I am captive still of my pleasant bands,
    The hands of a girl, and most your hands.

FLOS LUNAE

For YVANHOÉ RAMBOSSON

I would not alter thy cold eyes,
Nor trouble the calm fount of speech
With aught of passion or surprise.
The heart of thee I cannot reach:
I would not alter thy cold eyes!

I would not alter thy cold eyes;
Nor have thee smile, nor make thee weep:
Though all my life droops down and dies,
Desiring thee, desiring sleep,
I would not alter thy cold eyes.

I would not alter thy cold eyes;
I would not change thee if I might,
To whom my prayers for incense rise,
Daughter of dreams! my moon of night!
I would not alter thy cold eyes.

I would not alter thy cold eyes,
With trouble of the human heart:
Within their glance my spirit lies,
A frozen thing, alone, apart;
I would not alter thy cold eyes.

NON SUM QUALIS ERAM BONAE
SUB REGNO CYNARAE

Last night, ah, yesternight, betwixt her lips and mine
There fell thy shadow, Cynara! thy breath was shed
Upon my soul between the kisses and the wine;
And I was desolate and sick of an old passion,
    Yea, I was desolate and bowed my head:
I have been faithful to thee, Cynara! in my fashion.

All night upon mine heart I felt her warm heart beat,
Night-long within mine arms in love and sleep she lay;
Surely the kisses of her bought red mouth were sweet;
But I was desolate and sick of an old passion,
    When I awoke and found the dawn was gray:
I have been faithful to thee, Cynara! in my fashion.

I have forgot much, Cynara! gone with the wind,
Flung roses, roses riotously with the throng,
Dancing, to put thy pale, lost lilies out of mind;
But I was desolate and sick of an old passion,
    Yea, all the time, because the dance was long:
I have been faithful to thee, Cynara! in my fashion.

I cried for madder music and for stronger wine,
But when the feast is finished and the lamps expire,
Then falls thy shadow, Cynara! the night is thine;
And I am desolate and sick of an old passion,
    Yea hungry for the lips of my desire:
I have been faithful to thee, Cynara! in my fashion.

ERNEST DOWSON

(*From a drawing by Charles Conder*)

VANITAS

For VINCENT O'SULLIVAN

Beyond the need of weeping,
    Beyond the reach of hands,
May she be quietly sleeping,
    In what dim nebulous lands?
Ah, she who understands!

The long, long winter weather,
    These many years and days,
Since she, and Death, together,
    Left me the wearier ways:
And now, these tardy bays!

The crown and victor's token:
    How are they worth to-day?
The one word left unspoken,
    It were late now to say:
But cast the palm away!

For once, ah once, to meet her,
    Drop laurel from tired hands:
Her cypress were the sweeter,
    In her oblivious lands:
Haply she understands!

Yet, crossed that weary river,
  In some ulterior land,
Or anywhere, or ever,
  Will she stretch out a hand?
And will she understand?

EXILE

For Conal Holmes O'Connell O'Riordan

By the sad waters of separation
  Where we have wandered by divers ways,
I have but the shadow and imitation
  Of the old memorial days.

In music I have no consolation,
  No roses are pale enough for me;
The sound of the waters of separation
  Surpasseth roses and melody.

By the sad waters of separation
  Dimly I hear from an hidden place
The sigh of mine ancient adoration:
  Hardly can I remember your face.

If you be dead, no proclamation
  Sprang to me over the waste, gray sea:
Living, the waters of separation
  Sever for ever your soul from me.

No man knoweth our desolation;
  Memory pales of the old delight;
While the sad waters of separation
  Bear us on to the ultimate night.

SPLEEN

For ARTHUR SYMONS

I was not sorrowful, I could not weep,
And all my memories were put to sleep.

I watched the river grow more white and strange,
All day till evening I watched it change.

All day till evening I watched the rain
Beat wearily upon the window pane.

I was not sorrowful, but only tired
Of everything that ever I desired.

Her lips, her eyes, all day became to me
The shadow of a shadow utterly.

All day mine hunger for her heart became
Oblivion, until the evening came,

And left me sorrowful, inclined to weep,
With all my memories that could not sleep.

O MORS! QUAM AMARA EST MEMORIA TUA HOMINI PACEM HABENTI IN SUBSTANTIIS SUIS

Exceeding sorrow
  Consumeth my sad heart!
Because to-morrow
  We must depart,
Now is exceeding sorrow
  All my part!

Give over playing,
  Cast thy viol away:
Merely laying
  Thine head my way:
Prithee, give over playing,
  Grave or gay.

Be no word spoken;
  Weep nothing: let a pale
Silence, unbroken
  Silence prevail!
Prithee, be no word spoken,
  Lest I fail!

Forget to-morrow!
　Weep nothing: only lay
In silent sorrow
　Thine head my way:
Let us forget to-morrow,
　This one day!

Ah, dans ces mornes séjours
Les jamais sont les toujours.

PAUL VERLAINE

You would have understood me, had you waited;
   I could have loved you, dear! as well as he:
Had we not been impatient, dear! and fated
      Always to disagree.

What is the use of speech? Silence were fitter:
   Lest we should still be wishing things unsaid.
Though all the words we ever spake were bitter,
      Shall I reproach you dead?

Nay, let this earth, your portion, likewise cover
   All the old anger, setting us apart:
Always, in all, in truth was I your lover;
      Always, I held your heart.

I have met other women who were tender,
   As you were cold, dear! with a grace as rare.
Think you, I turned to them, or made surrender,
      I who had found you fair?

Had we been patient, dear! ah, had you waited,
   I had fought death for you, better than he:
But from the very first, dear! we were fated
      Always to disagree.

Late, late, I come to you, now death discloses
Love that in life was not to be our part:
On your low lying mound between the roses,
Sadly I cast my heart.

I would not waken you: nay! this is fitter;
Death and the darkness give you unto me;
Here we who loved so, were so cold and bitter,
Hardly can disagree.

APRIL LOVE

For ARTHUR CECIL HILLIER

We have walked in Love's land a little way,
　We have learnt his lesson a little while,
And shall we not part at the end of day,
　　With a sigh, a smile?

A little while in the shine of the sun,
　We were twined together, joined lips, forgot
How the shadows fall when the day is done,
　　And when Love is not.

We have made no vows—there will none be broke,
　Our love was free as the wind on the hill,
There was no word said we need wish unspoke,
　　We have wrought no ill.

So shall we not part at the end of day,
　Who have loved and lingered a little while,
Join lips for the last time, go our way,
　　With a sigh, a smile?

VAIN HOPE

Sometimes, to solace my sad heart, I say,
　Though late it be, though lily-time be past,
　Though all the summer skies be overcast,
Haply I will go down to her, some day,
　And cast my rests of life before her feet,
That she may have her will of me, being so sweet,
　　And none gainsay!

So might she look on me with pitying eyes,
　And lay calm hands of healing on my head:
　'Because of thy long pains be comforted;
For I, even I, am Love: sad soul, arise!'
　So, for her graciousness, I might at last
Gaze on the very face of Love, and hold Him fast
　　In no disguise.

Haply, I said, she will take pity on me,
　Though late I come, long after lily-time,
　With burden of waste days and drifted rhyme:
Her kind, calm eyes, down drooping maidenly,
　Shall change, grow soft: there yet is time, meseems,
I said, for solace; though I know these things are dreams
　　And may not be!

VAIN RESOLVES

I said: 'There is an end of my desire:
   Now have I sown, and I have harvested,
And these are ashes of an ancient fire,
   Which, verily, shall not be quickened.
Now will I take me to a place of peace,
      Forget mine heart's desire;
In solitude and prayer, work out my soul's release.

'I shall forget her eyes, how cold they were;
   Forget her voice, how soft it was and low,
With all my singing that she did not hear,
   And all my service that she did not know.
I shall not hold the merest memory
      Of any days that were,
Within those solitudes where I will fasten me.'

And once she passed, and once she raised her eyes,
   And smiled for courtesy, and nothing said:
And suddenly the old flame did uprise,
   And all my dead desire was quickened.
Yea! as it hath been, it shall ever be,
      Most passionless, pure eyes!
Which never shall grow soft, nor change, nor pity me.

A REQUIEM

For JOHN GRAY

Neobule, being tired,
Far too tired to laugh or weep,
From the hours, rosy and gray,
Hid her golden face away.
Neobule, fain of sleep,
Slept at last as she desired!

Neobule! is it well,
That you haunt the hollow lands,
Where the poor, dead people stray,
Ghostly, pitiful and gray,
Plucking, with their spectral hands,
Scentless blooms of asphodel?

Neobule, tired to death
Of the flowers that I threw
On her flower-like, fair feet,
Sighed for blossoms not so sweet,
Lunar roses pale and blue,
Lilies of the world beneath.

Neobule! ah, too tired
Of the dreams and days above!
Where the poor, dead people stray,
Ghostly, pitiful and gray,
Out of life and out of love,
Sleeps the sleep which she desired.

BEATA SOLITUDO

For SAM. SMITH

What land of Silence,
  Where pale stars shine
On apple-blossom
  And dew-drenched vine,
  Is yours and mine?

The silent valley
  That we will find,
Where all the voices
  Of humankind
  Are left behind.

There all forgetting,
  Forgotten quite,
We will repose us,
  With our delight
  Hid out of sight.

The world forsaken,
  And out of mind
Honour and labour,
  We shall not find
  The stars unkind.

And men shall travail,
　　And laugh and weep;
But we have vistas
　　Of gods asleep,
　　With dreams as deep.

A land of Silence,
　　Where pale stars shine
On apple-blossoms
　　And dew-drenched vine,
　　Be yours and mine!

TERRE PROMISE

For HERBERT P. HORNE

Even now the fragrant darkness of her hair
Had brushed my cheek; and once, in passing by,
Her hand upon my hand lay tranquilly:
What things unspoken trembled in the air!

Always I know, how little severs me
From mine heart's country, that is yet so far;
And must I lean and long across a bar,
That half a word would shatter utterly?

Ah might it be, that just by touch of hand,
Or speaking silence, shall the barrier fall;
And she shall pass, with no vain words at all,
But droop into mine arms, and understand!

AUTUMNAL

For ALEXANDER TEIXEIRA DE MATTOS

Pale amber sunlight falls across
   The reddening October trees,
   That hardly sway before a breeze
As soft as summer: summer's loss
   Seems little, dear! on days like these!

Let misty autumn be our part!
   The twilight of the year is sweet:
   Where shadow and the darkness meet
Our love, a twilight of the heart
   Eludes a little time's deceit.

Are we not better and at home
   In dreamful Autumn, we who deem
   No harvest joy is worth a dream?
A little while and night shall come,
   A little while, then, let us dream.

Beyond the pearled horizons lie
   Winter and night: awaiting these
   We garner this poor hour of ease,
Until love turn from us and die
   Beneath the drear November trees.

IN TEMPORE SENECTUTIS

When I am old,
  And sadly steal apart,
Into the dark and cold,
  Friend of my heart!
Remember, if you can,
Not him who lingers, but that other man,
Who loved and sang, and had a beating heart,—
  When I am old!

When I am old,
  And all Love's ancient fire
Be tremulous and cold:
  My soul's desire!
Remember, if you may,
Nothing of you and me but yesterday,
When heart on heart we bid the years conspire
    To make us old.

When I am old,
  And every star above
Be pitiless and cold:
  My life's one love!
Forbid me not to go:
Remember nought of us but long ago,
And not at last, how love and pity strove
    When I grew old!

VILLANELLE OF HIS LADY'S TREASURES

I took her dainty eyes, as well
    As silken tendrils of her hair:
And so I made a Villanelle!

I took her voice, a silver bell,
    As clear as song, as soft as prayer;
I took her dainty eyes as well.

It may be, said I, who can tell,
    These things shall be my less despair?
And so I made a Villanelle!

I took her whiteness virginal
    And from her cheek two roses rare:
I took her dainty eyes as well.

I said: 'It may be possible
    Her image from my heart to tear!'
And so I made a Villanelle.

I stole her laugh, most musical:
    I wrought it in with artful care;
I took her dainty eyes as well;
And so I made a Villanelle.

GRAY NIGHTS

For CHARLES SAYLE

Awhile we wandered (thus it is I dream!)
Through a long, sandy track of No Man's Land,
Where only poppies grew among the sand,
The which we, plucking, cast with scant esteem,
And ever sadlier, into the sad stream,
Which followed us, as we went, hand in hand,
Under the estrangèd stars, a road unplanned,
Seeing all things in the shadow of a dream.
And ever sadlier, as the stars expired,
We found the poppies rarer, till thine eyes
Grown all my light, to light me were too tired,
And at their darkening, that no surmise
Might haunt me of the lost days we desired,
After them all I flung those memories!

VESPERAL

For HUBERT CRACKANTHORPE

Strange grows the river on the sunless evenings!
The river comforts me, grown spectral, vague and dumb:
Long was the day; at last the consoling shadows come:
Sufficient for the day are the day's evil things!

Labour and longing and despair the long day brings;
Patient till evening men watch the sun go west;
Deferred, expected night at last brings sleep and rest:
Sufficient for the day are the day's evil things!

At last the tranquil Angelus of evening rings
Night's curtain down for comfort and oblivion
Of all the vanities observèd by the sun:
Sufficient for the day are the day's evil things!

So, some time, when the last of all our evenings
Crowneth memorially the last of all our days,
Not loth to take his poppies man goes down and says,
'Sufficient for the day were the day's evil things!'

THE GARDEN OF SHADOW

Love heeds no more the sighing of the wind
Against the perfect flowers: thy garden's close
Is grown a wilderness, where none shall find
One strayed, last petal of one last year's rose.

O bright, bright hair! O mouth like a ripe fruit!
Can famine be so nigh to harvesting?
Love, that was songful, with a broken lute
In grass of graveyards goeth murmuring.

Let the wind blow against the perfect flowers,
And all thy garden change and glow with spring:
Love is grown blind with no more count of hours,
Nor part in seed-time nor in harvesting.

SOLI CANTARE PERITI ARCADES

For AUBREY BEARDSLEY

Oh, I would live in a dairy,
    And its Colin I would be,
And many a rustic fairy
    Should churn the milk with me.

Or the fields should be my pleasure,
    And my flocks should follow me,
Piping a frolic measure
    For Joan or Marjorie.

For the town is black and weary,
    And I hate the London street;
But the country ways are cheery,
    And country lanes are sweet.

Good luck to you, Paris ladies!
    Ye are over fine and nice,
I know where the country maid is,
    Who needs not asking twice.

Ye are brave in your silks and satins,
    As ye mince about the Town;
But her feet go free in pattens,
    If she wear a russet gown.

If she be not queen nor goddess
  She shall milk my brown-eyed herds,
And the breasts beneath her bodice
  Are whiter than her curds.

So I will live in a dairy,
  And its Colin I will be,
And it's Joan that I will marry,
  Or, haply, Marjorie.

ON THE BIRTH OF A FRIEND'S CHILD

For VICTOR AND NELLIE PLARR

Mark the day white, on which the Fates have smiled:
Eugenio and Egeria have a child.
On whom abundant grace kind Jove imparts
If she but copy either parent's parts.
Then, Muses! long devoted to her race,
Grant her Egeria's virtues and her face;
Nor stop your bounty there, but add to it
Eugenio's learning and Eugenio's wit.

EXTREME UNCTION

For LIONEL JOHNSON

Upon the eyes, the lips, the feet,
  On all the passages of sense,
The atoning oil is spread with sweet
  Renewal of lost innocence.

The feet, that lately ran so fast
  To meet desire, are soothly sealed;
The eyes, that were so often cast
  On vanity, are touched and healed.

From troublous sights and sounds set free;
  In such a twilight hour of breath,
Shall one retrace his life, or see,
  Through shadows, the true face of death?

Vials of mercy! Sacring oils!
  I know not where nor when I come,
Nor through what wanderings and toils,
  To crave of you Viaticum.

Yet, when the walls of flesh grow weak,
  In such an hour, it well may be,
Through mist and darkness, light will break,
  And each anointed sense will see.

AMANTIUM IRAE

When this, our rose, is faded,
   And these, our days, are done,
In lands profoundly shaded
   From tempest and from sun:
Ah, once more come together,
   Shall we forgive the past,
And safe from worldly weather
   Possess our souls at last?

Or in our place of shadows
   Shall still we stretch an hand
To green, remembered meadows,
   Of that old pleasant land?
And vainly there foregathered,
   Shall we regret the sun?
The rose of love, ungathered?
   The bay, we have not won?

Ah, child! the world's dark marges
   May lead to Nevermore,
The stately funeral barges
   Sail for an unknown shore,
And love we vow to-morrow,
   And pride we serve to-day:
What if they both should borrow
   Sad hues of yesterday?

Our pride! Ah, should we miss it,
   Or will it serve at last?
Our anger, if we kiss it,
   Is like a sorrow past.
While roses deck the garden,
   While yet the sun is high,
Doff sorry pride for pardon,
   Or ever love go by.

IMPENITENTIA ULTIMA

For ROBERT HARBOROUGH SHERARD

Before my light goes out for ever if God should give me
    a choice of graces,
    I would not reck of length of days, nor crave for things
        to be;
But cry: 'One day of the great lost days, one face of all
    the faces,
    Grant me to see and touch once more and nothing
        more to see.

'For, Lord, I was free of all Thy flowers, but I chose the
    world's sad roses,
    And that is why my feet are torn and mine eyes are
        blind with sweat,
But at Thy terrible judgement-seat, when this my tired
    life closes,
    I am ready to reap whereof I sowed, and pay my
        righteous debt.

'But once before the sand is run and the silver thread
    is broken,
    Give me a grace and cast aside the veil of dolorous
        years,
Grant me one hour of all mine hours, and let me see for
    a token
    Her pure and pitiful eyes shine out, and bathe her
        feet with tears.'

Her pitiful hands should calm, and her hair stream down
     and blind me,
  Out of the sight of night, and out of the reach of fear,
And her eyes should be my light whilst the sun went out
     behind me,
  And the viols in her voice be the last sound in mine ear.

Before the ruining waters fall and my life be carried
     under,
  And Thine anger cleave me through as a child cuts
     down a flower,
I will praise Thee, Lord, in Hell, while my limbs are
     racked asunder,
  For the last sad sight of her face and the little grace
     of an hour.

A VALEDICTION

If we must part,
  Then let it be like this;
Not heart on heart,
  Nor with the useless anguish of a kiss;
But touch mine hand and say:
'*Until to-morrow or some other day,*
    If we must part.'

Words are so weak
  When love hath been so strong:
Let silence speak:
  '*Life is a little while, and love is long;*
A time to sow and reap,
And after harvest a long time to sleep,
    But words are weak.'

SAPIENTIA LUNAE

For ANDRÉ LEBEY

The wisdom of the world said unto me:
  '*Go forth and run, the race is to the brave;*
Perchance some honour tarrieth for thee!'
    'As tarrieth,' I said, 'for sure, the grave.'
      For I had pondered on a rune of roses,
      Which to her votaries the moon discloses.

The wisdom of the world said: '*There are bays:*
  Go forth and run, for victory is good,
After the stress of the laborious days.'
    'Yet,' said I, 'shall I be the worms' sweet food,'
      As I went musing on a rune of roses,
      Which in her hour, the pale, soft moon discloses.

Then said my voices: '*Wherefore strive or run,*
  On dusty highways ever, a vain race?
The long night cometh, starless, void of sun,
  What light shall serve thee like her golden face?'
    For I had pondered on a rune of roses,
    And knew some secrets which the moon discloses.

'Yea,' said I, 'for her eyes are pure and sweet
  As lilies, and the fragrance of her hair
Is many laurels; and it is not meet
    To run for shadows when the prize is here;'
      And I went reading in that rune of roses
      Which to her votaries the moon discloses.

Dum nos fata sinunt, oculos satiemus Amore.
PROPERTIUS

Cease smiling, Dear! a little while be sad,
　　Here in the silence, under the wan moon;
Sweet are thine eyes, but how can I be glad,
　　　　Knowing they change so soon?

For Love's sake, Dear, be silent! Cover me
　　In the deep darkness of thy falling hair:
Fear is upon me and the memory
　　　　Of what is all men's share.

O could this moment be perpetuate!
　　Must we grow old, and leaden-eyed and gray,
And taste no more the wild and passionate
　　　　Love sorrows of to-day?

Grown old, and faded, Sweet! and past desire,
　　Let memory die, lest there be too much ruth,
Remembering the old, extinguished fire
　　　　Of our divine, lost youth.

O red pomegranate of thy perfect mouth!
　　My lips' life-fruitage, might I taste and die,
Here in thy garden, where the scented south
　　　　Wind chastens agony;

Reap death from thy live lips in one long kiss,
   And look my last into thine eyes and rest:
What sweets had life to me sweeter than this
     Swift dying on thy breast?

Or, if that may not be, for Love's sake, Dear!
   Keep silence still, and dream that we shall lie,
Red mouth to mouth, entwined, and always hear
     The south wind's melody,

Here in thy garden, through the sighing boughs,
   Beyond the reach of time and chance and change,
And bitter life and death, and broken vows,
     That sadden and estrange.

SERAPHITA

Come not before me now, O visionary face!
Me tempest-tost, and borne along life's passionate sea;
Troublous and dark and stormy though my passage be;
Not here and now may we commingle or embrace,
Lest the loud anguish of the waters should efface
The bright illumination of thy memory,
Which dominates the night: rest, far away from me,
In the serenity of thine abiding-place!

But when the storm is highest, and the thunders blare,
And sea and sky are riven, O moon of all my night!
Stoop down but once in pity of my great despair,
And let thine hand, though over late to help, alight
But once upon my pale eyes and my drowning hair,
Before the great waves conquer in the last vain fight.

EPIGRAM

Because I am idolatrous and have besought,
With grievous supplication and consuming prayer,
The admirable image that my dreams have wrought
Out of her swan's neck and her dark, abundant hair:
The jealous gods, who brook no worship save their own,
Turned my live idol marble and her heart to stone.

QUID NON SPEREMUS, AMANTES?

For ARTHUR MOORE

Why is there in the least touch of her hands
  More grace than other women's lips bestow,
If love is but a slave in fleshly bands
  Of flesh to flesh, wherever love may go?

Why choose vain grief and heavy-hearted hours
  For her lost voice, and dear remembered hair,
If love may cull his honey from all flowers,
  And girls grow thick as violets, everywhere?

Nay! She is gone, and all things fall apart;
  Or she is cold, and vainly have we prayed;
And broken is the summer's splendid heart,
  And hope within a deep, dark grave is laid.

As man aspires and falls, yet a soul springs
  Out of his agony of flesh at last,
So love that flesh enthralls, shall rise on wings
  Soul-centred, when the rule of flesh is past.

Then, most High Love, or wreathed with myrtle sprays,
  Or crownless and forlorn, nor less a star,
Thee may I serve and follow, all my days,
  Whose thorns are sweet as never roses are!

CHANSON SANS PAROLES

In the deep violet air,
   Not a leaf is stirred;
   There is no sound heard,
But afar, the rare
   Trilled voice of a bird.

Is the wood's dim heart,
   And the fragrant pine,
   Incense, and a shrine
Of her coming? Apart,
   I wait for a sign.

What the sudden hush said,
   She will hear, and forsake,
   Swift, for my sake,
Her green, grassy bed:
   She will hear and awake!

She will hearken and glide,
   From her place of deep rest,
   Dove-eyed, with the breast
Of a dove, to my side:
   The pines bow their crest.

I wait for a sign:
   The leaves to be waved,
   The tall tree-tops laved
In a flood of sunshine,
   This world to be saved!

In the deep violet air,
   Not a leaf is stirred;
   There is no sound heard,
But afar, the rare
   Trilled voice of a bird.

DECORATIONS:

IN VERSE AND PROSE

BEYOND

Love's aftermath! I think the time is now
That we must gather in, alone, apart
The saddest crop of all the crops that grow,
     Love's aftermath.
Ah, sweet,—sweet yesterday, the tears that start
Can not put back the dial; this is, I trow,
Our harvesting! Thy kisses chill my heart,
Our lips are cold; averted eyes avow
The twilight of poor love: we can but part,
Dumbly and sadly, reaping as we sow,
     Love's aftermath.

IN VERSE

DE AMORE

Shall one be sorrowful because of love,
  Which hath no earthly crown,
  Which lives and dies, unknown?
Because no words of his shall ever move
  Her maiden heart to own
  Him lord and destined master of her own:
Is Love so weak a thing as this,
  Who can not lie awake,
  Solely for his own sake,
For lack of the dear hands to hold, the lips to kiss,
    A mere heart-ache?

Nay, though love's victories be great and sweet,
  Nor vain and foolish toys,
  His crowned, earthly joys,
Is there no comfort then in love's defeat?
  Because he shall defer,
  For some short span of years all part in her,
  Submitting to forego
  The certain peace which happier lovers know;
Because he shall be utterly disowned,
  Nor length of service bring
  Her least awakening:
Foiled, frustrate and alone, misunderstood, discrowned,
    Is Love less King?

103

Grows not the world to him a fairer place,
   How far soever his days
   Pass from his lady's ways,
From mere encounter with her golden face?
   Though all his sighing be vain,
   Shall he be heavy-hearted and complain?
Is she not still a star,
Deeply to be desired, worshipped afar,
   A beacon-light to aid
   From bitter-sweet delights, Love's masquerade?
Though he lose many things,
   Though much he miss:
The heart upon his heart, the hand that clings,
   The memorable first kiss;
Love that is love at all,
Needs not an earthly coronal;
Love is himself his own exceeding great reward,
     A mighty lord!

Lord over life and all the ways of breath,
   Mighty and strong to save
   From the devouring grave;
Yea, whose dominion doth out-tyrant death,
   Thou who art life and death in one,
   The night, the sun;
Who art, when all things seem:
   Foiled, frustrate and forlorn, rejected of to-day,
   Go with me all my way,
And let me not blaspheme.

THE DEAD CHILD

Sleep on, dear, now
  The last sleep and the best,
And on thy brow,
  And on thy quiet breast,
Violets I throw.

Thy scanty years
  Were mine a little while;
Life had no fears
  To trouble thy brief smile
With toil or tears.

Lie still, and be
  For evermore a child!
Not grudgingly,
  Whom life has not defiled,
I render thee.

Slumber so deep,
  No man would rashly wake;
I hardly weep,
  Fain only, for thy sake,
To share thy sleep.

Yes, to be dead,
   Dead, here with thee to-day,—
When all is said
   'Twere good by thee to lay
My weary head.

The very best!
   Ah, child so tired of play,
I stand confessed:
   I want to come thy way,
And share thy rest.

CARTHUSIANS

Through what long heaviness, assayed in what strange
    fire,
  Have these white monks been brought into the way of
    peace,
Despising the world's wisdom and the world's desire,
  Which from the body of this death bring no release?

Within their austere walls no voices penetrate;
  A sacred silence only, as of death, obtains;
Nothing finds entry here of loud or passionate;
  This quiet is the exceeding profit of their pains.

From many lands they came, in divers fiery ways;
  Each knew at last the vanity of earthly joys;
And one was crowned with thorns, and one was crowned
    with bays,
  And each was tired at last of the world's foolish noise.

It was not theirs with Dominic to preach God's holy
    wrath,
  They were too stern to bear sweet Francis' gentle sway;
Theirs was a higher calling and a steeper path,
  To dwell alone with Christ, to meditate and pray.

A cloistered company, they are companionless,
  None knoweth here the secret of his brother's heart:
They are but come together for more loneliness,
  Whose bond is solitude and silence all their part.

O beatific life! Who is there shall gainsay,
   Your great refusal's victory, your little loss,
Deserting vanity for the more perfect way,
   The sweeter service of the most dolorous Cross.

Ye shall prevail at last! Surely ye shall prevail!
   Your silence and austerity shall win at last:
Desire and mirth, the world's ephemeral lights shall fail,
   The sweet star of your queen is never overcast.

We fling up flowers and laugh, we laugh across the wine;
   With wine we dull our souls and careful strains of art;
Our cups are polished skulls round which the roses twine:
   None dares to look at Death who leers and lurks apart.

Move on, white company, whom that has not sufficed!
   Our viols cease, our wine is death, our roses fail:
Pray for our heedlessness, O dwellers with the Christ!
   Though the world fall apart, surely ye shall prevail.

THE THREE WITCHES

All the moon-shed nights are over,
  And the days of gray and dun;
There is neither may nor clover,
  And the day and night are one.

Not an hamlet, not a city
  Meets our strained and tearless eyes;
In the plain without a pity,
  Where the wan grass droops and dies.

We shall wander through the meaning
  Of a day and see no light,
For our lichened arms are leaning
  On the ends of endless night.

We, the children of Astarte,
  Dear abortions of the moon,
In a gay and silent party,
  We are riding to you soon.

Burning ramparts, ever burning!
  To the flame which never dies
We are yearning, yearning, yearning,
  With our gay and tearless eyes.

In the plain without a pity,
  (Not an hamlet, not a city)
  Where the wan grass droops and dies.

VILLANELLE OF THE POET'S ROAD

Wine and woman and song,
   Three things garnish our way:
Yet is day over long.

Lest we do our youth wrong,
   Gather them while we may:
Wine and woman and song.

Three things render us strong,
   Vine leaves, kisses and bay;
Yet is day over long.

Unto us they belong,
   Us the bitter and gay,
Wine and woman and song.

We, as we pass along,
   Are sad that they will not stay;
Yet is day over long.

Fruits and flowers among,
   What is better than they:
Wine and woman and song?
   Yet is day over long.

VILLANELLE OF ACHERON

By the pale marge of Acheron,
  Methinks we shall pass restfully,
Beyond the scope of any sun.

There all men hie them one by one,
  Far from the stress of earth and sea,
By the pale marge of Acheron.

'Tis well when life and love is done,
  'Tis very well at last to be,
Beyond the scope of any sun.

No busy voices there shall stun
  Our ears: the stream flows silently
By the pale marge of Acheron.

There is the crown of labour won,
  The sleep of immortality,
Beyond the scope of any sun.

Life, of thy gifts I will have none,
  My queen is that Persephone,
By the pale marge of Acheron,
  Beyond the scope of any sun.

SAINT GERMAIN-EN-LAYE
(1887–1895)

Through the green boughs I hardly saw thy face,
They twined so close: the sun was in mine eyes;
And now the sullen trees in sombre lace
Stand bare beneath the sinister, sad skies.

O sun and summer! Say in what far night,
The gold and green, the glory of thine head,
Of bough and branch have fallen? Oh, the white
Gaunt ghosts that flutter where thy feet have sped,

Across the terrace that is desolate,
And rang then with thy laughter, ghost of thee,
That holds its shroud up with most delicate,
Dead fingers, and behind the ghost of me,

Tripping fantastic with a mouth that jeers
At roseal flowers of youth the turbid streams
Toss in derision down the barren years
To death the host of all our golden dreams.

ERNEST DOWSON
(*From a drawing by Sir William Rothenstein*)

AFTER PAUL VERLAINE

I

Il pleut doucement sur la ville.
RIMBAUD

Tears fall within mine heart,
As rain upon the town:
Whence does this languor start,
Possessing all mine heart?

O sweet fall of the rain
Upon the earth and roofs!
Unto an heart in pain,
O music of the rain!

Tears that have no reason
Fall in my sorry heart:
What! there was no treason?
This grief hath no reason.

Nay! the more desolate,
Because, I know not why,
(Neither for love nor hate)
Mine heart is desolate.

AFTER PAUL VERLAINE

II

Colloque Sentimental

Into the lonely park all frozen fast,
Awhile ago there were two forms who passed.

Lo, are their lips fallen and their eyes dead,
Hardly shall a man hear the words they said.

Into the lonely park, all frozen fast,
There came two shadows who recall the past.

'Dost thou remember our old ecstasy?'—
'Wherefore should I possess that memory?'—

'Doth thine heart beat at my sole name alway?
Still dost thou see my soul in visions?' 'Nay!'—

'They were fair days of joy unspeakable,
Whereon our lips were joined?'—'I cannot tell.'—

'Were not the heavens blue, was not hope high?'—
'Hope has fled vanquished down the darkling sky.'—

So through the barren oats they wanderèd,
And the night only heard the words they said.

AFTER PAUL VERLAINE

III

SPLEEN

Around were all the roses red,
The ivy all around was black.

Dear, so thou only move thine head,
Shall all mine old despairs awake!

Too blue, too tender was the sky,
The air too soft, too green the sea.

Always I fear, I know not why,
Some lamentable flight from thee.

I am so tired of holly-sprays
And weary of the bright box-tree,

Of all the endless country ways;
Of everything alas! save thee.

AFTER PAUL VERLAINE

IV

The sky is up above the roof
    So blue, so soft!
A tree there, up above the roof,
    Swayeth aloft.

A bell within that sky we see,
    Chimes low and faint:
A bird upon that tree we see,
    Maketh complaint.

Dear God! is not the life up there,
    Simple and sweet?
How peacefully are borne up there
    Sounds of the street!

What hast thou done, who comest here,
    To weep alway?
Where hast thou laid, who comest here,
    Thy youth away?

TO HIS MISTRESS

There comes an end to summer,
　　To spring showers and hoar rime;
His mumming to each mummer
　　Has somewhere end in time,
And since life ends and laughter,
　　And leaves fall and tears dry,
Who shall call love immortal,
　　When all that is must die?

Nay, sweet, let's leave unspoken
　　The vows the fates gainsay,
For all vows made are broken,
　　We love but while we may.
Let's kiss when kissing pleases,
　　And part when kisses pall,
Perchance, this time to-morrow,
　　We shall not love at all.

You ask my love completest,
　　As strong next year as now,
The devil take you, sweetest,
　　Ere I make aught such vow.
Life is a masque that changes,
　　A fig for constancy!
No love at all were better,
　　Than love which is not free.

117

JADIS

Erewhile, before the world was old,
When violets grew and celandine,
In Cupid's train we were enrolled:
        Erewhile!
Your little hands were clasped in mine,
Your head all ruddy and sun-gold
Lay on my breast which was your shrine,
And all the tale of love was told:
Ah, God, that sweet things should decline,
And fires fade out which were not cold,
        Erewhile.

IN A BRETON CEMETERY

They sleep well here,
  These fisher-folk who passed their anxious days
  In fierce Atlantic ways;
And found not there,
  Beneath the long curled wave,
  So quiet a grave.

And they sleep well
  These peasant-folk, who told their lives away,
  From day to market-day,
As one should tell,
  With patient industry,
  Some sad old rosary.

And now night falls,
  Me, tempest-tost, and driven from pillar to post,
  A poor worn ghost,
This quiet pasture calls;
  And dear dead people with pale hands
  Beckon me to their lands.

TO WILLIAM THEODORE PETERS
ON HIS RENAISSANCE CLOAK

The cherry-coloured velvet of your cloak
  Time hath not soiled: its fair embroideries
Gleam as when centuries ago they spoke
  To what bright gallant of Her Daintiness,
  Whose slender fingers, long since dust and dead,
  For love or courtesy embroidered
The cherry-coloured velvet of this cloak.

Ah! cunning flowers of silk and silver thread,
  That mock mortality! the broidering dame,
The page they decked, the kings and courts are dead:
  Gone the age beautiful; Lorenzo's name,
  The Borgia's pride are but an empty sound;
  But lustrous still upon their velvet ground,
Time spares these flowers of silk and silver thread.

Gone is that age of pageant and of pride:
  Yet don your cloak, and haply it shall seem,
The curtain of old time is set aside;
  As through the sadder coloured throng you gleam;
  We see once more fair dame and gallant gay,
  The glamour and the grace of yesterday:
The elder, brighter age of pomp and pride.

THE SEA-CHANGE

Where river and ocean meet in a great tempestuous
    frown,
Beyond the bar, where on the dunes the white-capped
    rollers break;
Above, one windmill stands forlorn on the arid, grassy
    down:
I will set my sail on a stormy day and cross the bar and
    seek
That I have sought and never found, the exquisite one
    crown,
Which crowns one day with all its calm the passionate
    and the weak.

When the mad winds are unreined, wilt thou not storm,
    my sea?
(I have ever loved thee so, I have ever done thee
    wrong
In drear terrestrial ways.) When I trust myself to
    thee
With a last great hope, arise and sing thine ultimate,
    great song
Sung to so many better men, O sing at last to me,
That which when once a man has heard, he heeds not
    over long.

I will bend my sail when the great day comes; thy kisses
    on my face
Shall seal all things that are old, outworn; and anger
    and regret
Shall fade as the dreams and days shall fade, and in thy
    salt embrace,
When thy fierce caresses blind mine eyes and my limbs
    grow stark and set,
All that I know in all my mind shall no more have a
    place:
The weary ways of men and one woman I shall forget.

Point du Pouldu

DREGS

The fire is out, and spent the warmth thereof,
(This is the end of every song man sings!)
The golden wine is drunk, the dregs remain,
Bitter as wormwood and as salt as pain;
And health and hope have gone the way of love

Into the drear oblivion of lost things.
Ghosts go along with us until the end;
This was a mistress, this, perhaps, a friend.
With pale, indifferent eyes, we sit and wait
For the dropt curtain and the closing gate:
This is the end of all the songs man sings.

A SONG

All that a man may pray,
    Have I not prayed to thee?
What were praise left to say,
    Has not been said by me,
      O, ma mie?

Yet thine eyes and thine heart,
    Always were dumb to me:
Only to be my part,
    Sorrow has come from thee,
      O, ma mie?

Where shall I seek and hide
    My grief away with me?
Lest my bitter tears should chide,
    Bring brief dismay to thee,
      O, ma mie?

More than a man may pray,
    Have I not prayed to thee?
What were praise left to say,
    Has not been said by me,
      O, ma mie?

BRETON AFTERNOON

Here, where the breath of the scented-gorse floats
    through the sun-stained air,
On a steep hill-side, on a grassy ledge, I have lain hours
    long and heard
Only the faint breeze pass in a whisper like a prayer,
And the river ripple by and the distant call of a bird.

On the lone hill-side, in the gold sunshine, I will hush
    me and repose,
And the world fades into a dream and a spell is cast
    on me;
And what was all the strife about, for the myrtle or the
    rose,
And why have I wept for a white girl's paleness passing
    ivory!

Out of the tumult of angry tongues, in a land alone,
    apart,
In a perfumed dream-land set betwixt the bounds of
    life and death,
Here will I lie while the clouds fly by and delve an hole
    where my heart
May sleep deep down with the gorse above and red,
    red earth beneath.

Sleep and be quiet for an afternoon, till the rose-white
    angelus
Softly steals my way from the village under the hill:
Mother of God, O Misericord, look down in pity on us,
The weak and blind who stand in our light and wreak
    ourselves such ill.

VENITE DESCENDAMUS

Let be at last; give over words and sighing,
  Vainly were all things said:
Better at last to find a place for lying,
  Only dead.

Silence were best, with songs and sighing over;
  Now be the music mute;
Now let the dead, red leaves of autumn cover
  A vain lute.

Silence is best: for ever and for ever,
  We will go down and sleep,
Somewhere beyond her ken, where she need never
  Come to weep.

Let be at last: colder she grows and colder;
  Sleep and the night were best;
Lying at last where we can not behold her,
  We may rest.

TRANSITION

A little while to walk with thee, dear child;
  To lean on thee my weak and weary head;
Then evening comes: the winter sky is wild,
  The leafless trees are black, the leaves long dead.

A little while to hold thee and to stand,
  By harvest-field of bending golden corn:
Then the predestined silence, and thine hand,
  Lost in the night, long and weary and forlorn.

A little while to love thee, scarcely time
  To love thee well enough; then time to part,
To fare through wintry fields alone and climb
  The frozen hills, not knowing where thou art.

Short summer-time and then, my heart's desire,
  The winter and the darkness: one by one
The roses fall, the pale roses expire
  Beneath the slow decadence of the sun.

EXCHANGES

All that I had I brought,
　Little enough I know;
A poor rhyme roughly wrought,
　A rose to match thy snow:
All that I had I brought.

Little enough I sought:
　But a word compassionate,
A passing glance, or thought,
　For me outside the gate:
Little enough I sought.

Little enough I found:
　All that you had, perchance!
With the dead leaves on the ground,
　I dance the devil's dance.
　All that you had I found.

TO A LADY ASKING FOOLISH QUESTIONS

Why am I sorry, Chloe? Because the moon is far:
And who am I to be straitened in a little earthly star?

Because thy face is fair? And what if it had not been,
The fairest face of all is the face I have not seen.

Because the land is cold, and however I scheme and plot,
I can not find a ferry to the land where I am not.

Because thy lips are red and thy breasts upbraid the
    snow?
(There is neither white nor red in the pleasance where
    I go.)

Because thy lips grow pale and thy breasts grow dun
    and fall?
I go where the wind blows, Chloe, and am not sorry
    at all.

RONDEAU

Ah, Manon, say, why is it we
Are one and all so fain of thee?
Thy rich red beauty debonnaire
In very truth is not more fair,
Than the shy grace and purity
That clothe the maiden maidenly;
Her gray eyes shine more tenderly
And not less bright than thine her hair,
    Ah, Manon, say!
Expound, I pray, the mystery
Why wine-stained lip and languid eye,
And most unsaintly Maenad air,
Should move us more than all the rare
White roses of virginity?
Ah, Manon, say!

MORITURA

A song of the setting sun!
  The sky in the west is red,
And the day is all but done:
  While yonder up overhead,
    All too soon,
There rises, so cold, the cynic moon.

A song of a winter day!
  The wind of the north doth blow,
From a sky that's chill and gray,
  On fields where no crops now grow,
    Fields long shorn
Of bearded barley and golden corn.

A song of an old, old man!
  His hairs are white and his gaze,
Long bleared in his visage wan,
  With its weight of yesterdays,
    Joylessly
He stands and mumbles and looks at me.

A song of a faded flower!
  'Twas plucked in the tender bud,
And fair and fresh for an hour,
  In a lady's hair it stood.
    Now, ah, now,
Faded it lies in the dust and low.

LIBERA ME

Goddess the laughter-loving, Aphrodite befriend!
Long have I served thine altars, serve me now at the
    end,
Let me have peace of thee, truce of thee, golden one,
    send.

Heart of my heart have I offered thee, pain of my pain,
Yielding my life for the love of thee into thy chain;
Lady and goddess be merciful, loose me again.

All things I had that were fairest, my dearest and best,
Fed the fierce flames on thine altar: ah, surely, my
    breast
Shrined thee alone among goddesses, spurning the rest.

Blossom of youth thou hast plucked of me, flower of my
    days;
Stinted I nought in thine honouring, walked in thy
    ways,
Song of my soul pouring out to thee, all in thy praise.

Fierce was the flame while it lasted, and strong was thy
    wine,
Meet for immortals that die not, for throats such as
    thine,
Too fierce for bodies of mortals, too potent for mine.

Blossom and bloom hast thou taken, now render to me
Ashes of life that remain to me, few though they be,
Truce of the love of thee, Cyprian, let me go free.

Goddess, the laughter-loving, Aphrodite, restore
Life to the limbs of me, liberty, hold me no more
Having the first-fruits and flower of me, cast me the
core.

TO A LOST LOVE

I seek no more to bridge the gulf that lies
  Betwixt our separate ways;
  For vainly my heart prays,
Hope droops her head and dies;
I see the sad, tired answer in your eyes.

I did not heed, and yet the stars were clear;
  Dreaming that love could mate
  Lives grown so separate;—
But at the best, my dear,
I see we should not have been very near.

I knew the end before the end was nigh:
  The stars have grown so plain;
  Vainly I sigh, in vain
For things that come to some,
But unto you and me will never come.

WISDOM

Love wine and beauty and the spring,
  While wine is red and spring is here,
And through the almond blossoms ring
  The dove-like voices of thy Dear.

Love wine and spring and beauty while
  The wine hath flavour and spring masks
Her treachery in so soft a smile
  That none may think of toil and tasks.

But when spring goes on hurrying feet,
  Look not thy sorrow in the eyes,
And bless thy freedom from thy sweet:
  This is the wisdom of the wise.

IN SPRING

See how the trees and the osiers lithe
Are green bedecked and the woods are blithe,
The meadows have donned their cape of flowers
The air is soft with the sweet May showers,
   And the birds make melody:
But the spring of the soul, the spring of the soul,
   Cometh no more for you or for me.

The lazy hum of the busy bees
Murmureth through the almond trees;
The jonquil flaunteth a gay, blonde head,
The primrose peeps from a mossy bed,
   And the violets scent the lane.
But the flowers of the soul, the flowers of the soul,
   For you and for me bloom never again.

A LAST WORD

Let us go hence: the night is now at hand;
The day is overworn, the birds all flown;
And we have reaped the crops the gods have sown;
Despair and death; deep darkness o'er the land,
Broods like an owl; we cannot understand
Laughter or tears, for we have only known
Surpassing vanity: vain things alone
Have driven our perverse and aimless band.
Let us go hence, somewhither strange and cold,
To Hollow Lands where just men and unjust
Find end of labour, where's rest for the old,
Freedom to all from love and fear and lust.
Twine our torn hands! O pray the earth enfold
Our life-sick hearts and turn them into dust.

IN PROSE

THE FORTUNATE ISLANDS

Bearded, with tawny faces, as they sat on the quay, looking listlessly at nothing with their travelled eyes, I questioned them:

'We have adventured,' they said.

'Tell me of your travels, O mariners, of that you have sought and found, of high perils undergone and great salvage and of those fortunate islands which lie in a quiet sea, azure beyond my dreaming.'

'We have found nothing. There is nothing saved,' they said.

'But tell me, O mariners, for I have travelled a little. I have looked for the woman I might have loved, and the friend we hear of, and the country where I am not. Tell me of your discoveries.'

One of them answered:

'We tell you the truth. We are old, withered mariners, and long and far have we wandered in the seas of no discovery. We have been to the end of the last ocean, but there was nothing, not even the things of which you speak. We have adventured, but we have not found anything, and here we are again in the port of our nativity, and there is only one thing we expect. Is it not so, comrades?'

Each raised a hand of asseveration; and they said:

'We tell you the truth: there are no fortunate islands.'

And they fell into their old silence.

MARKETS

AFTER AN OLD NURSERY RHYME

'Where are you going, beautiful maiden?'

'I am going to market, sir.'

'And what do you take with you, beautiful maiden? Lilies out of your garden? White milk, warm from the cow, little pats of yellow butter, new-laid eggs, this morning's mushrooms? Where is your basket? Why have you nothing in your hands?'

'I am going to market, sir.'

'Beautiful maiden, may I come with you?'

'Oh, sir.'

ABSINTHIA TAETRA

Green changed to white, emerald to an opal: nothing was changed.

The man let the water trickle gently into his glass, and as the green clouded, a mist fell away from his mind.

Then he drank opaline.

Memories and terrors beset him. The past tore after him like a panther and through the blackness of the present he saw the luminous tiger eyes of the things to be.

But he drank opaline.

And that obscure night of the soul, and the valley of humiliation, through which he stumbled were forgotten. He saw blue vistas of undiscovered countries, high prospects and a quiet, caressing sea. The past shed its perfume over him, to-day held his hand as it were a little child, and to-morrow shone like a white star: nothing was changed.

He drank opaline.

The man had known the obscure night of the soul, and lay even now in the valley of humiliation; and the tiger menace of the things to be was red in the skies. But for a little while he had forgotten.

Green changed to white, emerald to an opal: nothing was changed.

THE VISIT

As though I were still struggling through the meshes of some riotous dream, I heard his knock upon the door. As in a dream, I bade him enter, but with his entry, I awoke. Yet when he entered it seemed to me that I was dreaming, for there was nothing strange in that supreme and sorrowful smile which shone through the mask which I knew. And just as though I had not always been afraid of him I said: 'Welcome.'

And he said very simply, 'I am here.'

Dreaming I had thought myself, but the reproachful sorrow of his smile showed me that I was awake. Then dared I open my eyes and I saw my old body on the bed, and the room in which I had grown so tired, and in the middle of the room the pan of charcoal which still smouldered. And dimly I remembered my great weariness and the lost whiteness of Lalage and last year's snows; and these things had been agonies.

Darkly, as in a dream, I wondered why they gave me no more hurt, as I looked at my old body on the bed; why, they were like old maids' fancies (as I looked at my gray body on the bed of my agonies)—like silly toys of children that fond mothers lay up in lavender (as I looked at the twisted limbs of my old body), for these things had been agonies.

But all my wonder was gone when I looked again into the eyes of my guest, and I said:

'I have wanted you all my life.'

Then said Death (and what reproachful tenderness
was shadowed in his obscure smile):
'You had only to call.'

THE PRINCESS OF DREAMS

Poor legendary princess! In her enchaunted tower of ivory, the liberator thought that she awaited him.

For once in a dream he had seen, as they were flowers de luce, the blue lakes of her eyes, had seemed to be enveloped in a tangle of her golden hair.

And he sought her through the countless windings of her forest for many moons, sought her through the morasses, sparing not his horse nor his sword. On his way he slew certain evil magicians and many of his friends, so that at his journey's end his bright sword was tarnished and his comeliness swart with mud. His horses he had not spared: their bones made a white track behind him in the windings of the forest: but he still bore her ransom, all the costly, graceful things stored in a cypress chest: massed pearls and amethysts and silks from Samarcand, Valance of Venice, and fine tapestry of Tyre. All these he brought with him to the gates of her ivory tower.

Poor legendary princess.

For he did not free her and the fustian porter took his treasure and broke his stained sword in two.

And who knows where he went, horseless and disarmed, through the morasses and the dark windings of her forest under the moonless night, dreaming of those blue lakes which were flowers de luce, her eyes? Who knows? For the fustian porter says nothing, being slow of wit.

But there are some who say that she had no wish to be freed, and that those flowers de luce, her eyes, are a stagnant, dark pool, that her glorious golden hair was only long enough to reach her postern gate.

Some say, moreover, that her tower is not of ivory and that she is not even virtuous nor a princess.

THE PIERROT
OF THE MINUTE

A DRAMATIC PHANTASY
IN ONE ACT

THE CHARACTERS

A Moon Maiden
Pierrot

THE SCENE

A glade in the Parc du Petit Trianon. In the centre a Doric temple with steps coming down the stage. On the left a little Cupid on a pedestal. Twilight.

[Enter Pierrot, carrying lilies. He
stands gazing at the Temple de l'Am

Pierrot My journey's end! This surely is the glade,
That ~~which~~ I was promised: I have well obeyed!
A clue of lilies was I bid to find,
Where the green alleys most obscurely wind;
Where tall oaks darkliest canopy o'erhead,
And moss and violet make ~~the silent~~ a softer bed;
Where the path ends, and leagues behind one lie
The ~~glowing~~ courts and pleachèd gardens of Versailles.
The lilies streamed before me, green and white;
I gathered, following: they led me right;
To ~~rearing~~ the bright temple and ~~the~~ sacred grove
This is, in truth, the very Shrine of Love.

        [He lays his flowers before Cupid's
          Statue: then he goes timidly up the
          steps to the temple.]

It is so solitary, I grow afraid:
Is there no priest here, or devoted maid?
Is there no oracle, no voice to speak,
Interpreting to me, the word I seek?

THE FIRST SHEET OF THE *PIERROT* MANUSCRIPT
(*From the original MS in the possession of Lessing Rosenwald*)

(Pierrot enters with his hands full of lilies. He is
burdened with a little basket. He stands gazing
at the Temple and the Statue.)

Pierrot.

    My journey's end! This surely is the glade
Which I was promised: I have well obeyed!
A clue of lilies was I bid to find,
Where the green alleys most obscurely wind;
Where tall oaks darkliest canopy o'erhead,
And moss and violet make the softest bed;
Where the path ends, and leagues behind me lie
The gleaming courts and gardens of Versailles;
The lilies streamed before me, green and white;
I gathered, following; they led me right,   10
To the bright temple and the sacred grove:
This is, in truth, the very shrine of Love!

(He gathers together his flowers and lays them
at the foot of Cupid's statue; then he goes timidly
up the first steps of the temple and stops.)

Pierrot.

    It is so solitary, I grow afraid.
Is there no priest here, no devoted maid?
Is there no oracle, no voice to speak,
Interpreting to me the word I seek?

(A very gentle music of lutes floats out from the
temple. Pierrot starts back; he shows extreme

151

surprise; then he returns to the foreground, and
crouches down in rapt attention until the music
ceases. His face grows puzzled and petulant.)

Pierrot.

Too soon! too soon! in that enchanting strain,
Days yet unlived, I almost lived again:
It almost taught me that I most would know—
Why am I here, and why am I Pierrot?　　　　20

(Absently he picks up a lily which has fallen to
the ground, and repeats:)

Pierrot.

Why came I here, and why am I Pierrot?
That music and this silence both affright;
Pierrot can never be a friend of night.
I never felt my solitude before—
Once safe at home, I will return no more.
Yet the commandment of the scroll was plain;
While the light lingers let me read again.

(He takes a scroll from his bosom and reads:)

Pierrot.

'*He loves to-night who never loved before;*
Who ever loved, to-night shall love once more.'
I never loved! I know not what love is.
I am so ignorant—but what is this?

(Reads)
'Who would adventure to encounter Love
Must rest one night within this hallowed grove.
Cast down thy lilies, which have led thee on,
Before the tender feet of Cupidon.'
Thus much is done, the night remains to me.
Well, Cupidon, be my security!
Here is more writing, but too faint to read.

(He puzzles for a moment, then casts the scroll down.)

Pierrot.

    Hence, vain old parchment. I have learnt thy
      rede!

(He looks round uneasily, starts at his shadow; then discovers his basket with glee. He takes out a flask of wine, pours it into a glass, and drinks.)

Pierrot.

    Courage, mon Ami! I shall never miss   40
Society with such a friend as this.
How merrily the rosy bubbles pass,
Across the amber crystal of the glass.
I had forgotten you. Methinks this quest
Can wake no sweeter echo in my breast.

(Looks round at the statue, and starts.)

Pierrot.

> Nay, little god! forgive. I did but jest.

(He fills another glass, and pours it upon the
statue.)

Pierrot.

>> This libation, Cupid, take,
>>> With the lilies at thy feet;
>> Cherish Pierrot for their sake
>>> Send him visions strange and sweet,   50
>> While he slumbers at thy feet.
>> Only love kiss him awake!
>> *Only love kiss him awake!*

(Slowly falls the darkness, soft music plays,
while Pierrot gathers together fern and foliage
into a rough couch at the foot of the steps which
lead to the Temple d'Amour. Then he lies down
upon it, having made his prayer. It is night.)

Pierrot. (Softly.)

> Music, more music, far away and faint:
> It is an echo of mine heart's complaint.
> Why should I be so musical and sad?
> I wonder why I used to be so glad?
> In single glee I chased blue butterflies,
> Half butterfly myself, but not so wise,
> For they were twain, and I was only one.   60
> Ah me! how pitiful to be alone.

My brown birds told me much, but in mine ear
They never whispered this—I learned it here:
The soft wood sounds, the rustlings in the breeze,
Are but the stealthy kisses of the trees.
Each flower and fern in this enchanted wood
Leans to her fellow, and is understood;
The eglantine, in loftier station set,
Stoops down to woo the maidly violet.
In gracile pairs the very lilies grow:
None is companionless except Pierrot.
Music, more music! how its echoes steal
Upon my senses with unlooked for weal.
Tired am I, tired, and far from this lone glade
Seems mine old joy in rout and masquerade.
Sleep cometh over me, now will I prove,
By Cupid's grace, what is this thing called love.

(Sleeps.)
(There is more music of lutes for an interval,
during which a bright radiance, white and cold,
streams from the temple upon the face of
Pierrot. Presently a Moon Maiden steps out of
the temple; she descends and stands over the
sleeper.)

The Lady.
        Who is this mortal
        Who ventures to-night
        To woo an immortal,   80
        Cold, cold the moon's light,

For sleep at this portal,
Bold lover of night.
Fair is the mortal
In soft, silken white,
Who seeks an immortal.
Ah, lover of night,
Be warned at the portal,
And save thee in flight!

(She stoops over him: Pierrot stirs in his sleep.)

Pierrot (Murmuring).
Forget not, Cupid. Teach me all thy lore:
'*He loves to-night who never loved before.*'

The Lady.
Unwitting boy! when, be it soon or late,
What Pierrot ever has escaped his fate?
What if I warned him! He might yet evade,
Through the long windings of this verdant glade;
Seek his companions in the blither way,
Which, else, must be as lost as yesterday.
So might he still pass some unheeding hours
In the sweet company of birds and flowers.
How fair he is, with red lips formed for joy,   100
As softly curved as those of Venus' boy.
Methinks his eyes, beneath their silver sheaves,
Rest tranquilly like lilies under leaves.
Arrayed in innocence, what touch of grace
Reveals the scion of a courtly race?

Well, I will warn him, though, I fear, too late—
What Pierrot ever has escaped his fate?
But, see, he stirs, new knowledge fires his brain,
And Cupid's vision bids him wake again.
Dione's Daughter! but how fair he is,   110
Would it be wrong to rouse him with a kiss?

(She stoops down and kisses him, then withdraws into the shadow.)

Pierrot (Rubbing his eyes).
    Celestial messenger! remain, remain;
Or, if a vision, visit me again!
What is this light, and whither am I come
To sleep beneath the stars so far from home?

(Rises slowly to his feet.)

Pierrot.
    Stay, I remember this is Venus' Grove,
And I am hither come to encounter——

The Lady (Coming forward, but veiled).
                          Love!

Pierrot (In ecstasy, throwing himself at her feet).
    Then have I ventured and encountered Love?

The Lady.
    Not yet, rash boy! and, if thou wouldst be wise, 120
Return unknowing; he is safe who flies.

Pierrot.

> Never, sweet lady, will I leave this place
> Until I see the wonder of thy face.
> Goddess or Naiad! lady of this Grove,
> Made mortal for a night to teach me love,
> Unveil thyself, although thy beauty be
> Too luminous for my mortality.

The Lady (Unveiling).

> Then, foolish boy, receive at length thy will:
> Now knowest thou the greatness of thine ill.

Pierrot.

> Now have I lost my heart, and gained my goal. 130

The Lady.

> Didst thou not read the warning on the scroll?

Pierrot (Picking up the parchment).

> I read it all, as on this quest I fared,
> Save where it was illegible and hard.

The Lady.

> Alack! poor scholar, wast thou never taught
> A little knowledge serveth less than naught?
> Hadst thou perused——but, stay, I will explain
> What was the writing which thou didst disdain.

(Reads)
> '*Au Petit Trianon*, at night's full noon,
> Mortal, beware the kisses of the moon!
> Whoso seeks her she gathers like a flower—   140
> He gives a life, and only gains an hour.'

Pierrot (Laughing recklessly).
> Bear me away to thine enchanted bower,
> All of my life I venture for an hour.

The Lady.
> Take up thy destiny of short delight;
> I am thy lady for a summer's night.
> Lift up your viols, maidens of my train,
> And work such havoc on this mortal's brain
> That for a moment he may touch and know
> Immortal things, and be full Pierrot.
> White music, Nymphs! Violet and Eglantine!   150
> To stir his tired veins like magic wine.
> What visitants across his spirit glance,
> Lying on lilies, while he watch me dance?
> Watch, and forget all weary things of earth,
> All memories and cares, all joy and mirth,
> While my dance wooes him, light and rythmical,
> And weaves his heart into my coronal.
> Music, more music for his soul's delight:
> Love is his lady for a summer's night.

(Pierrot reclines, and gazes at her while she
dances. The dance finished, she beckons to him:
he rises dreamily, and stands at her side.)

Pierrot.

    Whence came, dear Queen, such magic melody? 160

The Lady.

    Pan made it long ago in Arcady.

Pierrot.

    I heard it long ago, I know not where,
As I knew thee, or ever I came here.
But I forget all things—my name and race,
All that I ever knew except thy face.
Who art thou, lady? Breathe a name to me,
That I may tell it like a rosary.
Thou, whom I sought, dear Dryad of the trees,
How art thou designate—art thou Heart's-Ease?

The Lady.

    Waste not the night in idle questioning,   170
Since Love departs at dawn's awakening.

Pierrot.

    Nay, thou art right; what recks thy name or state,
Since thou art lovely and compassionate.
Play out thy will on me: I am thy lyre.

The Lady.

    I am to each the face of his desire.

Pierrot.

 I am not Pierrot, but Venus' dove,
Who craves a refuge on the breast of love.

The Lady.

 What wouldst thou of the maiden of the moon?
Until the cock crow I may grant thy boon.

Pierrot.

 Then, sweet Moon Maiden, in some magic
car,   180
Wrought wondrously of many a homeless star—
Such must attend thy journeys through the
skies,—
Drawn by a team of milk-white butterflies,
Whom, with soft voice and music of thy maids,
Thou urgest gently through the heavenly glades;
Mount me beside thee, bear me far away
From the low regions of the solar day;
Over the rainbow, up into the moon,
Where is thy palace and thine opal throne;
There on thy bosom——   190

The Lady.   Too ambitious boy!
I did but promise thee one hour of joy.
This tour thou plannest, with a heart so light,
Could hardly be completed in a night.
Hast thou no craving less remote than this?

Pierrot.

    Would it be impudent to beg a kiss?

The Lady.

    I say not that: yet prithee have a care!
    Often audacity has proved a snare.
    How wan and pale do moon-kissed roses grow—
    Dost thou not fear my kisses, Pierrot?   200

Pierrot.

    As one who faints upon the Libyan plain
    Fears the oasis which brings life again!

The Lady.

    Where far away green palm trees seem to stand
    May be a mirage of the wreathing sand.

Pierrot.

    Nay, dear enchantress, I consider naught,
    Save mine own ignorance, which would be
    taught.

The Lady.

    Dost thou persist?

Pierrot.   I do entreat this boon!

(She bends forward, their lips meet: she
withdraws with a petulant shiver. She utters a
peal of clear laughter.)

162

The Lady.
>   Why art thou pale, fond lover of the moon?

Pierrot.
>   Cold are thy lips, more cold than I can tell;   210
>   Yet would I hang on them, thine icicle!
>   Cold is thy kiss, more cold than I could dream
>   Arctus sits, watching the Boreal stream:
>   But with its frost such sweetness did conspire
>   That all my veins are filled with running fire;
>   Never I knew that life contained such bliss
>   As the divine completeness of a kiss.

The Lady.
>   Apt scholar! so love's lesson has been taught,
>   Warning, as usual, has gone for naught.

Pierrot.
>   Had all my schooling been of this soft kind,   220
>   To play the truant I were less inclined.
>   Teach me again! I am a sorry dunce—
>   I never knew a task by conning once.

The Lady.
>   Then come with me! below this pleasant shrine
>   Of Venus we will presently recline,
>   Until birds' twitter beckon me away
>   To mine own home, beyond the milky-way.
>   I will instruct thee, for I deem as yet
>   O Love thou knowest but the alphabet.

Pierrot.

In its sweet grammar I shall grow most wise, 230
If all its rules be written in thine eyes.

(The lady sits upon a step of the temple, and
Pierrot leans upon his elbow at her feet, regard-
ing her.)

Pierrot.

Sweet contemplation! how my senses yearn
To be thy scholar always, always learn.
Hold not so high from me thy radiant mouth,
Fragrant with all the spices of the South;
Nor turn, O sweet! thy golden face away,
For with it goes the light of all my day.
Let me peruse it, till I know by rote
Each line of it, like music, note by note;
Raise thy long lashes, Lady! smile again: 240
These studies profit me.

(Taking her hand.)

The Lady.   Refrain, refrain!

Pierrot (With passion).

I am but studious, so do not stir;
Thou art my star, I thine astronomer!
Geometry was founded on thy lip.

(Kisses her hand.)

The Lady.
> This attitude becomes not scholarship!
> Thy zeal I praise; but, prithee, not so fast,
> Nor leave the rudiments until the last.
> Science applied is good, but t'were a schism
> To study such before the catechism.   250
> Bear thee more modestly, while I submit
> Some easy problems to confirm thy wit.

Pierrot.
> In all humility my mind I pit
> Against her problems which would test my wit.

The Lady (Questioning him from a little book bound deliciously in vellum).
>> What is Love?
> Is it a folly,
> Is it mirth, or melancholy?
>> Joys above,
> Are there many, or not any?
> What is love?   260

Pierrot (Answering in a very humble attitude of scholarship).
>> If you please,
>> A most sweet folly!
> Full of mirth and melancholy:
>> Both of these!
> In its sadness worth all gladness,
>> If you please!

165

The Lady.

> Prithee where,
> Goes Love a-hiding?
> Is he long in his abiding
> Anywhere?   270
> Can you bind him when you find him;
> Prithee, where?

Pierrot.

> With spring days
> Love comes and dallies:
> Upon the mountains, through the valleys
> Lie Love's ways.
> Then he leaves you and deceives you
> In spring days.

The Lady.

> Thine answers please me: 'tis thy turn to ask.
> To meet thy questioning be now my task.   280

Pierrot.

> Since I know thee, dear Immortal,
> Is my heart become a blossom,
> To be worn upon thy bosom.
> When thou turn me from this portal,
> Whither shall I, hapless mortal,
> Seek love out and win again
> Heart of me that thou retain?

The Lady.

    In and out the woods and valleys,
Circling, soaring like a swallow,
Love shall flee and thou shalt follow: 290
Though he stops awhile and dallies,
Never shalt thou stay his malice!
Moon-kissed mortals seek in vain
To possess their hearts again!

Pierrot.

    Tell me, Lady, shall I never
Rid me of this grievous burden!
Follow Love and find his guerdon
In no maiden whatsoever?
Wilt thou hold my heart for ever?
Rather would I thine forget,   300
In some earthly Pierrette!

The Lady.

    Thus thy fate, whate'er thy will is!
Moon-struck child, go seek my traces
Vainly in all mortal faces!
In and out among the lilies,
Court each rural Amaryllis:
Seek the signet of Love's hand
In each courtly Corisande!

Pierrot.

    Now, verily, sweet maid, of school I tire:
These answers are not such as I desire.   310

167

The Lady.
>Why art thou sad?

Pierrot.   I dare not tell.

The Lady (Caressingly).   Come, say!

Pierrot.
>Is love all schooling, with no time to play?

The Lady.
>Though all love's lessons be a holiday,
>Yet I will humour thee: what wouldst thou play?

Pierrot.
>What are the games that small moon-maids
>   enjoy,
>Or is their time all spent in staid employ?

The Lady.
>Sedate they are, yet games they much enjoy:
>They skip with stars, the rainbow is their toy.   320

Pierrot.
>That is too hard!

The Lady.   For mortal's play.

Pierrot.   What then?

The Lady.
>Teach me some pastime from the world of men.

Pierrot.
> I have it, maiden.

The Lady. Can it soon be taught?

Pierrot.
> A simple game, I learnt it at the Court.
> I sit by thee.

The Lady. But, prithee, not so near.

Pierrot.
> That is essential, as will soon appear. 330
> Lay here thine hand, which cold night dews anoint,
> Washing its white——

The Lady. Now is this to the point?

Pierrot.
> Prithee, forbear! Such is the game's design.

The Lady.
> Here is my hand.

Pierrot. I cover it with mine.

The Lady.
> What must I next?

> (They play.)

Pierrot.   Withdraw.

The Lady.   It goes too fast.

(They continue playing, until Pierrot catches her hand.)

Pierrot (Laughing).
    'Tis done. I win my forfeit at the last.   340

(He tries to embrace her. She escapes; he chases her round the stage; she eludes him.)

The Lady.
    Thou art not quick enough. Who hopes to catch
    A moon-beam, must use twice as much despatch.

Pierrot (Sitting down sulkily).
    I grow aweary, and my heart is sore.
    Thou dost not love me; I will play no more.

(He buries his face in his hands: the lady stands over him.)

The Lady.
    What is this petulance?

Pierrot.   'Tis quick to tell—
    Thou hast but mocked me.

The Lady.   Nay! I love thee well!

170

Pierrot.

    Repeat those words, for still within my breast
    A whisper warns me they are said in jest.   350

The Lady.

    I jested not: at daybreak I must go,
    Yet loving thee far better than thou know.

Pierrot.

    Then, by this altar, and this sacred shrine,
    Take my sworn troth, and swear thee wholly
        mine!
    The gods have wedded mortals long ere this.

The Lady.

    There was enough betrothal in my kiss.
    What need of further oaths?

Pierrot.   That bound not thee!

The Lady.

    Peace! since I tell thee that it may not be.
    But sit beside me whilst I soothe thy bale   360
    With some moon fancy or celestial tale.

Pierrot.

    Tell me of thee, and that dim, happy place
    Where lies thine home, with maidens of thy
        race!

171

The Lady (Seating herself).

> Calm is it yonder, very calm; the air
> For mortals' breath is too refined and rare;
> Hard by a green lagoon our palace rears
> Its dome of agate through a myriad years.
> A hundred chambers its bright walls enthrone,
> Each one carved strangely from a precious stone.
> Within the fairest, clad in purity,   370
> Our mother dwelleth immemorially:
> Moon-calm, moon-pale, with moon stones on
>   her gown
> The floor she treads with little pearls is sown;
> She sits upon a throne of amethysts,
> And orders mortal fortunes as she lists;
> I, and my sisters, all around her stand,
> And, when she speaks, accomplish her demand.

Pierrot.

> Methought grim Clotho and her sisters twain
> With shrivelled fingers spun this web of bane!

The Lady.

> Their's and my mother's realm is far apart;   380
> Her's is the lustrous kingdom of the heart,
> And dreamers all, and all who sing and love,
> Her power acknowledge, and her rule approve.

Pierrot.

> Me, even me, she hath led into this grove.

The Lady.
    Yea, thou art one of hers! But, ere this night,
Often I watched my sisters take their flight
Down heaven's stairway of the clustered stars
To gaze on mortals through their lattice bars;
And some in sleep they woo with dreams of bliss
Too shadowy to tell, and some they kiss.   390
But all to whom they come, my sisters say,
Forthwith forget all joyance of the day,
Forget their laughter and forget their tears,
And dream away with singing all their years—
Moon-lovers always!

    (She sighs.)

Pierrot.   Why art sad, sweet Moon?

    (Laughing.)

The Lady.
    For this, my story, grant me now a boon.

Pierrot.
    I am thy servitor.

The Lady.   Would, then, I knew
More of the earth, what men and women do.   400

Pierrot.
    I will explain.

The Lady.   Let brevity attend
   Thy wit, for night approaches to its end.

Pierrot.
      Once was I a page at Court, so trust in me:
   That's the first lesson of society.

The Lady.
      Society?

Pierrot.   I mean the very best
   Pardy! thou wouldst not hear about the rest.
   I know it not, but am a *petit maître*
   At rout and festival and *bal champêtre*.   410
   But since example be instruction's ease,
   Let's play the thing.—Now, Madame, if you please!

(He helps her to rise, and leads her forward:
then he kisses her hand, bowing over it with a
very courtly air.)

The Lady.
      What am I, then?

Pierrot.   A most divine Marquise!
   Perhaps that attitude hath too much ease.

(Passes her.)

Ah, that is better! To complete the plan,
Nothing is necessary save a fan.

The Lady.

 Cool is the night, what needs it?

Pierrot.   Madame, pray

 Reflect, it is essential to our play.   420

The Lady (Taking a lily).

 Here is my fan!

Pierrot.   So, use it with intent:

 The deadliest arm in beauty's armament!

The Lady.

 What do we next?

Pierrot.   We talk!

The Lady.   But what about?

Pierrot.

 We quiz the company and praise the rout;
 Are polished, petulant, malicious, sly,
 Or what you will, so reputations die.
 Observe the Duchess in Venetian lace,   430
 With the red eminence.

The Lady.   A pretty face!

Pierrot.

> For something tarter set thy wits to search—
> 'She loves the churchman better than the church.'

The Lady.

> Her blush is charming; would it were her own!

Pierrot.

> Madame is merciless!

The Lady.   Is that the tone?

Pierrot.

> The very tone: I swear thou lackest naught,
> Madame was evidently bred at Court.

The Lady.

> Thou speakest glibly: 'tis not of thine age.   440

Pierrot.

> I listened much, as best becomes a page.

The Lady.

> I like thy Court but little——

Pierrot.   Hush! the Queen!
> Bow, but not low—thou knowest what I mean.

The Lady.

> Nay, that I know not!

Pierrot. Though she wear a crown,
'Tis from La Pompadour one fears a frown.

The Lady.
Thou art a child: thy malice is a game.

Pierrot.
A most sweet pastime—scandal is its name.

The Lady.
Enough, it wearies me.   450

Pierrot. Then, rare Marquise,
Desert the crowd to wander through the trees.

(He bows low, and she curtsies; they move
round the stage. When they pass before the
Statue he seizes her hand and falls on his knee.)

The Lady.
What wouldst thou now?

Pierrot. Ah, prithee, what, save thee!

The Lady.
Was this included in thy comedy?

Pierrot.
Ah, mock me not! In vain with quirk and jest
I strive to quench the passion in my breast;

In vain thy blandishments would make me play:
Still I desire far more than I can say.
My knowledge halts, ah, sweet, be piteous,   460
Instruct me still, while time remains to us,
Be what thou wist, Goddess, moon-maid, *Marquise*,
So that I gather from thy lips heart's ease,
Nay, I implore thee, think thee how time flies!

The Lady.
    Hush! I beseech thee, even now night dies.

Pierrot.
    Night, day, are one to me for thy soft sake.

(He entreats her with imploring gestures, she
hesitates: then puts her finger on her lip,
hushing him.)

The Lady.
    It is too late, for hark! the birds awake.

Pierrot.
    The birds awake! It is the voice of day!

The Lady.
    Farewell, dear youth! They summon me away.

(The light changes, it grows daylight: and music
imitates the twitter of the birds. They stand
gazing at the morning: then Pierrot sinks back
upon his bed, he covers his face in his hands.)

The Lady (Bending over him).

    Music, my maids! His weary senses steep
In soft untroubled and oblivious sleep,   470
With mandragore anoint his tirèd eyes,
That they may open on mere memories,
Then shall a vision seem his lost delight,
With love, his lady for a summer's night.
Dream thou hast dreamt all this, when thou
      awake,
Yet still be sorrowful, for a dream's sake.
I leave thee, sleeper! Yea, I leave thee now,
Yet take my legacy upon thy brow:
Remember me, who was compassionate,
And opened for thee once, the ivory gate.   480
I come no more, thou shalt not see my face
When I am gone to mine exalted place:
Yet all thy days are mine, dreamer of dreams,
All silvered over with the moon's pale beams:
Go forth and seek in each fair face in vain,
To find the image of thy love again.
All maids are kind to thee, yet never one
Shall hold thy truant heart till day be done.
Whom once the moon has kissed, loves long and
      late,
Yet never finds the maid to be his mate.   490
Farewell, dear sleeper, follow out thy fate.

(The Moon Maiden withdraws: a song is sung
from behind: it is full day.)

179

THE MOON MAIDEN'S SONG

Sleep! Cast thy canopy
   Over this sleeper's brain,
Dim grow his memory,
   When he awake again.

Love stays a summer night,
   Till lights of morning come;
Then takes her wingèd flight
   Back to her starry home.

Sleep! Yet thy days are mine;   **500**
   Love's seal is over thee:
Far though my ways from thine,
   Dim though thy memory.

Love stays a summer night,
   Till lights of morning come;
Then takes her wingèd flight
   Back to her starry home.

(When the song is finished, the curtain falls
upon Pierrot sleeping.)

NOTES

A KEY TO RECURRENT REFERENCES
IN THE NOTES

FLOWER, DESMOND: *The Poetical Works of Ernest Christopher Dowson*, London, 1934, appears as *Flower*.

LONGAKER, MARK: *Ernest Dowson*, a Biography, Philadelphia, 2nd ed., 1945, appears as *Longaker*.

PLARR, VICTOR: *Ernest Dowson 1888–1897: Reminiscences, Unpublished Letters and Marginalia, with a Bibliography Compiled by H. Guy Harrison*, London, 1914, as *Plarr*.

SYMONS, ARTHUR: *The Poems of Ernest Dowson, with a Memoir by Arthur Symons*, London, 1905. Page references to 1929 reprint. Appears as *Symons*.

I

VERSES

Verses, which appeared in the spring of 1896, was Dowson's first volume of poems. It was issued by Leonard Smithers[1] in a small printing of three hundred copies on handmade paper and thirty copies on Japanese vellum. The binding block was done by Aubrey Beardsley.[2] At the time the book appeared, the poet was fairly well known

[1] For the publication of his poems, Dowson had made some tentative arrangements with John Lane; and Lane and Elkin Mathews, who had published his collection of stories *Dilemmas* in the fall of 1895, assumed that the volume of poems would be theirs to issue when Dowson had submitted enough verse to make a sufficiently sizable book. The arrangements, however, had been interrupted by Dowson's distracting experiences over his parents' death and by his journey into Flanders and his life in Paris. In the meantime, his literary fortunes had become so much involved with the House of Smithers that all thought of publication began and ended at Arundel Street. Smithers, pleased with Dowson's contributions to the *Savoy* and the translations the poet was making for him from the French, encouraged Dowson to get his verse together and promised to issue it to his advantage (*Longaker*, p. 199). His decision to let Smithers have the poems instead of Lane and Mathews gave him concern. "I am afraid H—— is annoyed with me because I have published my verses out of the series." (*Plarr*, p. 117.) It is possible that Lane and Mathews would have published the poems to Dowson's greater advantage.

[2] Beardsley's binding block, which Dowson liked very much, the artist considered a joke, probably because he disliked Dowson. The two curves of the block formed a letter Y, the interpretation of which, Beardsley told his friends, was easy to determine: "Why was this book ever written?" (*Longaker*, p. 186.)

in literary circles through his contributions to *London Society*, the *Century Guild Hobby Horse*, and the first and second *Book of the Rhymers' Club* (1892 and 1894). As early as 1891, he and Victor Plarr, and possibly Lionel Johnson, had planned a joint volume, but the project was never carried out. The late appearance of a volume devoted entirely to his own poems was the result of Dowson's modesty and indecision rather than to any lack of material. As early as 1892 he had carefully written out eighty-eight poems in a manuscript book which he had started in 1886, in which the entries are dated, with indications of the periodicals in which some of them had been printed. (*Flower*, pp. 237 ff.) He drew on this manuscript book, which he called his "Poésie Schublade," not only for many of the poems in *Verses* but also for some of the poems in his second volume, *Decorations: In Verse and Prose* (1899).

A considerable number of the poems in *Verses* bore dedications to the poet's friends, a practice more in favor at the time than later, and for which in his case he probably had the precedent of Verlaine. The inscriptions range from names of those whom Dowson had known for many years to those who were little more than passing acquaintances. In only a very few instances were the poems written directly to and for the persons to whom they were inscribed. In fact, some of the poems which bear dedications had been written long before the poet had even heard of the men and women to whom they were inscribed; and the relationship of the poem to the person seems at times quite remote. Even to one who has studied Dowson's life and letters carefully there are names among the motley list which cannot be identified. His acquaintanceship in Paris during 1895–1896 while he was deliberating over names for the dedications was evidently quite large, for in a letter to Edgar Jepson written late in 1895, he said with an unusual lack of modesty: "I know a heap of persons and get as many cards for private views as if I were a celebrity." (*Longaker*, p. 195.)

The exact number of author's copies which Smithers yielded cannot be determined, but there were not enough to cover the dedication list, for some of the men to whom poems had been inscribed were not favored with a presentation copy.

When the book finally appeared, Dowson was much pleased with it. In a letter to Sam Smith dated "In:fest: Corp:Christi" 1896, he wrote: "I am glad you like the volume. Do you like Aubrey Beardsley's binding block? I am very pleased with it. There are no reviews yet, but I have had charming letters from [John] Gray, Teixeira [de Mattos] and [Arthur] Symons, the last of whom, as also Yeats, are going to write about it." (*Longaker*, p. 202.) The review that Yeats was going to write apparently was never done, and the notice of Arthur Symons did not appear until the August issue of the *Savoy*, at which time the editor devoted three pages to the circumstances of Dowson's life rather than to his *Verses* in an article entitled "A Literary Causerie." The London newspapers were prompter in their recognition, and the notices were generally favorable. The *Daily Chronicle*, for instance, reported: "Mr. Dowson has genuine talent. A classic propriety of epithet, rising at moments to a remarkable distinction; a full, rich melody, and . . . an occasional dignity of thought and feeling." (*Longaker*, p. 203.)

An underlying unity in *Verses* has been detected by some readers, notably his Oxford friend W. R. Thomas, who felt that the poems in the volume constitute a cycle "whose unity needs emphasizing. Two numbers, *Soli Cantare* and *A Friend's Child* have crept in by mischance, but, when these are removed, a sequence of intimate verses remains that can hardly be paralleled. Shakespeare's *Sonnets*, Meredith's *Modern Love*, and Housman's *Shropshire Lad* are all artificial beside this real thing." ("Ernest Dowson at Oxford," *The Nineteenth Century*, April, 1928.) Thomas's opinion in this instance is definitely subject to question. There are poems other than "Soli Cantare" and "A Friend's Child" which seem to be irrelevant to the unity which Thomas detected. The fact remains, however, that the poems in the volume were carefully selected and arranged.

"IN PREFACE: FOR ADELAIDE"

The dedicatory epistle, dated from Pont-Aven, Finistère, 1896, was written when Dowson's attachment for Adelaide Foltinowicz was at its height. He had met her in the fall of 1891, when she was only twelve, in her father's restaurant, 19 Sherwood Street, Soho, a cheap but entirely respectable eating place which he and his friends called "Poland." The passage in French, drawn from Gustave Flaubert's *Education sentimentale*, would seem to indicate that the girl was sufficiently conversant with the French to justify its use in the epistle. Reports vary about her appearance and whether she was worthy of the poet's devotion. Dark-haired and blue-eyed, with a nose that observers other than Dowson found a little crooked, she was quite as decorative and gentle-mannered as many a poet's inamorata. Edgar Jepson remembered her long oval face, its warm coloring, and the beauty of freshness and youth. "Poets have sung of poorer loves," he remarked. Although Dowson must have found her features attractive, it was not her beauty which appealed to him, for to her comeliness he rarely referred. It was her unspoiled, unaffected grace and sincerity which arrested and held his attention. In spite of her rearing in a neighborhood in which the English of Oxford was rarely heard, she had no trace of cockney in her speech, but spoke with an accent that came from her association with her parents, which gave a note of piquancy and quaintness to her talk. Her innocent prattle gave Dowson immeasurable delight. He was not alone in recognizing the girl's charm, for the other patrons, including Jepson and Langdale, liked the girl, and often beckoned her away from the table at the rear to come to talk with them. It was Langdale who started to call her "Missie".

Conal O'Riordan, however, among many others, had different reports. To the present editor, O'Riordan said: "Dowson's attitude toward the *Geliebte* was of course pure fantasy, and his death I consider to have been less a disaster than his marriage to her (were it conceivable) must have proved . . . the little restaurant where dwelt his *Geliebte* had an atmosphere of garlic in which I could not have drunk a cup of coffee. . . ." (*Longaker*, p. 188.) Missie married Auguste, a waiter in her father's restaurant in September, 1897, a little more than a year after the epistle was addressed to her. (*Plarr*, p. 123.)

Dowson was much concerned about the responses of both Adelaide and his friends to the Preface. "The very future day" of which he spoke so wistfully never came. The object of the dedication wrote to him fairly often after its appearance, but they were "friendly letters." Plarr evidently did not like the epistle, for Dowson stated uneasily: "Perhaps you are right in your remarks about my Preface." (*Longaker*, p. 202.) To Sam Smith he wrote in March: "I hope the dedication will be understood of her and accepted—and although there is no name, nor initials even—it will doubtless be understood of others—who will not, I hope, think it extravagant. It is very literally true." In a later letter: "Let me know how you find them [the poems], and if you think the 'Preface' is indiscreet." (John Gawsworth, "The Dowson Legend," *Transactions of the Royal Society of Literature*, March 24, 1939, p. 121.)

Although Dowson himself gave support to the notion that Adelaide was the ultimate source of the inspiration of all his poetry, that all he said in the Preface was "literally true," it is scarcely reasonable to conclude that Dowson's poetry was entirely the result of this attachment. Arthur Symons' inquiry: "Did it ever mean very much to her to have made and to have killed a poet?" (*Symons*, p. xiii) is plainly an oversimplification. Dowson wrote much poetry before he knew Missie, nor did his inspiration cease after the attachment was broken. It was, however, of great significance to him as a man and as a poet; and many of the lines of his life and talent converged in his love for Adelaide.

VITAE SUMMA BREVIS SPEM NOS VETAT INCOHARE LONGAM.

First printed in *Verses* (1896). Since the poem does not appear in Dowson's manuscript book, and no versions or references to it are encountered before its appearance in *Verses*, one might conclude that it was written immediately before the poems were sent to the publisher as a sort of epigraph to the volume. The tone of the poem, furthermore, indicates that it could well be concurrent with the composition of the prose "In Preface: For Adelaide." The title, drawn from Horace, *Odes*, Book I: iv, line 15, can be rendered freely as "Life's brief span forbids long enduring hope." Poe's poem "A Dream within a Dream," with its lines

> All that we see or seem
> Is but a dream within a dream

with which Dowson was no doubt familiar, is an interesting parallel.

1. A CORONAL

With His songs and Her days to His Lady and to Love

This poem was first printed as the first poem in *Verses* (1896). It was originally intended for a little volume which he and Victor Plarr planned to issue and was perhaps the only poem which Dowson, according to his own report, "ever wrote straight off in less than an hour." Lionel Johnson was possibly to have been a third contributor to the intended volume. In an undated letter to Plarr, written sometime in the autumn of 1891, he inquired: "Seriously—what of my suggestion concerning the mutual-of-some-of-our-poems-presently-publication question? If you don't mind! at least if we can't do it now, we might select about twenty, ten of yours & ten of mine, arrange them, get a happy title—have them typed and discover what the cost would be. A thin little booklet of some twenty-four pages would contain them— ought not to cost more than £10. Perhaps Image would design us a cover. Give this your attention. Roses and Rue by two authors. Or Suaviola or Vine Leaves and Violets or 'Apple Blossoms from Oxford.' " In a letter written a week or so later, he continued:

Mon cher Vieux,

Thanks for yours; the spirit in which you accept my suggestion is precisely my own; £10 is a chimerical sum to me; but let us prepare our garland for the day (surely it must come) when this impecunious tyranny is over worn. Of the titles I like not much the Teutonic ones; they are quaint but not harmonious. Best seem Suaviola or Gossamer—as affording least handle to the banality of critics: better I like 'Vineleaf & Violet'—and best perhaps 'Rose and Pine'—both of which titles would certainly drive the same critics wild. . . . I have been looking over my 'Poesie Schublade' as represented by a small MSS book and it will be with difficulty that I shall find ten worthy of the company of the best of yours. I shall bring up about 15 if I can of the least bad & you shall reject five. . . .

Appended to this letter were the three stanzas of "A

Coronal" which Dowson was to use, with a few changes in the wording and punctuation, as the first poem in *Verses*. (*Longaker*, pp. 111–112.)

Plarr, recalling in 1914 the intended volume, observed: "The search for pretty and rather absurd titles was more fashionable twenty years ago than now." (*Plarr*, p. 80.) Mere prettiness was hardly Dowson's objective in suggesting such titles as "Suaviola" and "Vineleaf and Violet." His sensitive ear is everywhere in evidence in both his verse and prose. His fondness for the *v* sound he often expressed. Arthur Symons recalled his saying that he considered the line, "The viol, the violet, and the vine" from Poe's poem "The City in the Sea" of surpassing beauty, (*Symons*, p. xxv.)

An interesting contemporary reference to Dowson's expressed fondness for the *v* sound is found in a sonnet by Patricio Gannon, the celebrated Argentinian poet, which appeared in the December, 1947, issue of *La Nación*.

ELEGIA PARA ERNEST DOWSON

"the viol, the violet and the vine"
(Verso de Poe que Dowson admiraba)

Ernest Dowson poet enamorado
de la muy venturosa V del vino,
vanagloria visual, verso vedado,
vaporoso velero bizantino.

Mágica letra V que ha desterrado
la ingrácil U en el misal latino,
voz de la tarde vaga que ha volcado
una V en el bifúrquico camino.

V de la vocación de antifonero
que en el vano vacío de un domingo
de vaguedad al vulgo vocinglero;

pálidas voces novias de un poeta
sois apenas tres sombras que distingo
en la viola, la viña y la violeta.

2. NUNS OF THE PERPETUAL ADORATION

First appeared in the *Century Guild Hobby Horse* (October, 1891) under the title "The Carmelite Nuns of the Perpetual Adoration," along with "Flos Lunae" and "Amor Umbratilis," the three poems grouped under the title "In Praise of Solitude." Henry Davray had the poem printed in the *Mercure de France* in March, 1892, with an accompanying French translation. It appeared again as one of Dowson's contributions to the first *Book of the Rhymers' Club* (1892), and then appeared as Number 2 in *Verses*, with slight changes in wording and punctuation.

It is one of Dowson's few devotional poems, written in the winter of 1891 at the time he was trying to condition himself for his conversion to Catholicism. A great deal of nonsense has been written about Dowson's conversion to the Catholic faith. When Frank Harris reported that Dowson had told him, "I am for the old faith. I've become a Catholic, as every artist must," he gave support to the belief that Dowson found little more than a sensuous beauty in the Church. In a letter to the present editor, Robert Sherard observed: "I always understood that Ernest 'verted' while at Oxford as so many young men of his generation did. . . . It was the picturesqueness of the Roman ritual that attracted him, but he never in his last years ensued his religion or confessed, or communicated. . . ." Plarr was more outspoken than was usual for him when he recalled his friend's conversion and the reasons underlying it. "I shall never forget the day of his admittance to the Church," wrote Plarr. "He came to me rather excitedly, and yet shook hands with weak indecision. . . . 'I have been admitted,' he said, but he seemed disappointed, for the heavens had not fallen, nor had a sign been vouchsafed. The priest who had admitted him had done so quite casually and had seemed bored. Afterwards, it seemed to me he forgot about his religion with surprising alacrity. Only his poetry bears witness to a romantic admiration of a creed, which, after all, he shares with many Protestants and Agnostics." (*Longaker*, pp. 68–69.) Yeats in *The Trembling of the Veil* reflected: "Dowson's poetry shows how sincerely he felt the fascination of religion, but his religion certainly had no dogmatic outline, being but a condition of virginal ecstasy. If it is true, as Arthur Symons, his very close friend, has written, that he loved the restaurant-keeper's daughter for her youth, one may be almost certain that he sought from religion some similar quality, something of that which the angels find who move perpetually, as Swedenborg has said, towards 'the day spring of their youth.' "

If his conversion seemed to have had only a few superficial effects to his friends, it had a perceptible bearing on the content and manner of his writing; and no one who examines understandingly "The Nuns of the

Perpetual Adoration" and his other devotional poems can fail to feel Dowson's urgent need for the sanctuary from life and from himself which the Church afforded. He sought no mystical revelation. It was enough for him to be aware of the Nunc Dimittis.

The theme and mood of the poem appear in expanded form in Dowson's prose tale, "Apple Blossom in Brittany," which appeared in the *Yellow Book*, for October, 1894. The nuns in the tale are Ursulines, an order with which Dowson identified the nuns in two of his early versions of the poem. (*Flower*, p. 245.)

I have been unable to identify the Countess Sobieska von Platt to whom the poem is inscribed. By the time the poem appeared in 1896 in *Verses*, Dowson's female acquaintanceship was fairly wide and varied. The obviously Polish part of the name might suggest an acquaintance whom the poet knew through his association with the Foltinowicz family, although Adelaide's station in life would scarcely bear out such an identification.

3. VILLANELLE OF SUNSET

First printed in the first *Book of the Rhymers' Club* (1892), and included as Number 3 in *Verses* with changes in the punctuation. This was one of the poems which led Yeats to feel that the best work of the members of the Rhymers' Club should be collected into a permanent volume. In recalling his reasons for proposing the book, he paid Dowson a very fine tribute. "For long, I only knew Dowson's *O Mors*, to quote but the first words of its long title, and *Villanelle of Sunset* from his reading, and it was because of the desire to hold them in my hand that I suggested the first *Book of the Rhymers' Club.* They were not speech, but perfect song, though song for the speaking voice." (*The Autobiography of William Butler Yeats: The Trembling of the Veil,* New York, 1958, p. 200.)

Only 350 copies of the first *Book of the Rhymers' Club* were issued by Elkin Mathews and John Lane. Nine of the ninety-four pages in the volume were given to Dowson—six poems in all, the maximum allowed to any one member. Of the members represented in the first book, only Dowson, Yeats, Johnson, Rhys, and Greene had so many. (For a detailed consideration of the Rhymers' Club, see Yeats's essay, "The Tragic Generation," in *The Autobiography of William Butler Yeats* and his account in *The Listener,* October 14, 1936; Ernest Rhys's *Everyman Remembers,* London, 1931; Richard Le Gallienne's *The Romantic Nineties,* London, 1926; and Mark Longaker, "The Rhymers' Club," *Ernest Dowson,* 2nd ed., Philadelphia, 1945.)

4. MY LADY APRIL

One of Dowson's early poems, it was written in the spring of 1888, and first printed in *Temple Bar* in April, 1889. Included as Number 4 in *Verses* with a few changes in wording and punctuation, none of which alters the theme and mood of the poem. Dowson told Arthur Moore that the editor of *Temple Bar* had paid him a guinea for the poem. (Dowson-Moore correspondence, April, 1889, Morgan Library Collection.) At the time the poem was written, Dowson was especially devoted to the sonnet form, a pattern in which he worked with considerable skill. The rhyme scheme in this sonnet is conventional enough—*abba abba cdcd dc*,—despite its variation in the sestet; but in his use of half-rhyme in the *c* line of the sestet with the *a* line of the octet he attained an unusual and pleasing tonal effect.

Léopold Nelkin, to whom the poem was dedicated, was one of Dowson's acquaintances in Paris in 1895–1896. Contrary to Flower's identification, Nelkin was probably a Russian, not a Pole. Dowson was familiar enough with Poles to know the difference. In a letter to Henry Davray, written sometime during the spring of 1896, the poet wrote: "I am glad you have come across Léopold Nelkin. C'est un charmant garçon with a particularly suave and gentle manner, which I find essentially Russian." Nelkin was probably not too good company for Dowson, for in a later letter to Davray, he wrote: "Do you ever see Léopold Nelkin? My friend Smith seems to have had a most debauched and frivolous quinzaine under his ciceronage." Again to Davray: "I have left your books and also one of Lautrec's with my Russian friend Léopold. . . ." (*Longaker*, pp. 198, 277, 279.)

5. TO ONE IN BEDLAM

Appeared first in the *Albemarle*, August, 1892; reprinted in the second *Book of the Rhymers' Club* (1894), and included as Number 5 in *Verses*. Henry Davray, to whom the poem was dedicated, liked it sufficiently to plan to translate it into French for the *Mercure de*

France, a plan which was apparently never carried out. Arthur Symons selected the poem for special comment: "Here, in the moment's intensity of this comradeship with madness, observe how beautiful the whole thing becomes; how instinctively the imagination of the poet turns what is sordid into a radiance, all stars and flowers and the divine part of forgetfulness! It is a symbol of the two sides of his own life: the side open to the street, and the side turned away from it, where he could 'hush and bless himself with silence.' " (*Symons*, p. xxvii.)

Henry Davray, to whom the poem is inscribed, was a fluently bilingual intermediary between the English and French writers of the nineties. As an editor of the *Mercure de France* he did much to make his French readers aware and appreciative of what the younger English poets were doing in both London and Paris. Of Dowson's verse he was especially fond, and the poet evidently had a high regard for Davray's taste. In a letter to Davray, written in the spring of 1896, Dowson said: "It is charming of you to write about me in your series. Any 'documents' you may require I shall be delighted to send you." And in a later letter: "Just a line to thank you very much for the reviews & mags. . . . Thank you also immensely for your offer to write of my poems in the 'Hermitage.' " (*Longaker*, pp. 278–279.)

6. AD DOMNULAM SUAM

Appeared originally in the first *Book of the Rhymers' Club* (1892), and included as Number 6 in *Verses*. In Dowson's manuscript book, which he often referred to as his "Poesie Schublade," the poem is dated Oct. 18, 1890. (*Flower*, p. 248.) It is one of Dowson's many poems in which there is a celebration of innocence, a theme which occupied much of his attention even as early as November, 1886, at which time there appeared in *London Society* a sonnet entitled "To a Little Girl." Who the "Little Lady" of his heart was, or the "Little Girl" of the earlier sonnet, cannot be determined; although we do not know exactly when Dowson's fondness for the little Polish girl Adelaide Foltinowicz began, it is reasonable to conclude that it was not until the early nineties, when he was already down from college for some time, and hence the "Little Lady" was not Adelaide, if she was a particular little girl at all. That the poet did not need a particular little girl as an object and motive for writing about the beauty of innocence is given support by recalling Edgar Jepson's remark that there was a cult of little girls at Oxford during the eighties. (*Memories of a Victorian*, London, 1933, Vol. I, p. 112.) If one were so inclined, one could present a considerable list of literary men of the late nineteenth century who were unable to resist the unaffected charm of little girls, and who gave expression in prose and verse to their pleasure in being with them and contemplating their innocence. Guy Harrison, in compiling a list of Dowson's works for Victor Plarr's *Ernest Dowson* (1914), lists among the poet's contributions to the short-lived *Critic* "The Cult of the Child." Dowson's title to the poem is an interesting instance of his use of Latin. "Domnulam," which I have been unable to find elsewhere in Latin love poetry, can be translated as a sort of affectionate diminutive—dear little mistress.

7. AMOR UMBRATILIS

Appeared originally in the *Century Guild Hobby Horse*, October, 1891, again in the first *Book of the Rhymers' Club* (1892), and was included as Number 7 in *Verses*. According to Plarr, the poem was one of the first pieces "that attracted much attention. It was published, if I remember rightly, by Mr. Herbert Horne in the *Century Guild Hobby Horse* together with a batch of the poet's other most noteworthy verses. The MS. of it, in pencil, lies before me now, inscribed on the back of a fierce letter referring to the poet's Oxford bills, which, he told me, he had agreed to pay by degrees. 'You have not returned the promissory note as arranged—please do so at once.' And Ernest Dowson has immortalized this gruffness with one of the loveliest elegies in the language! One wonders if he chose his scrap of paper of set purpose. The solicitor's date on it is October 7, 1890." (*Plarr*, p. 19.) It is possible, as Plarr stated, that this was "one of the first poems which attracted much attention," but it seems reasonable to conclude that Dowson had already aroused considerable interest in his work in the preceding April issue of the *Hobby Horse*, for it was in that issue that there appeared for the first time the justly famous "Non sum qualis eram bonae sub regno Cynarae." Dowson himself thought well of "Amor Umbratilis," for he sent copies of it not only to Plarr, but also to other friends, including Arthur Moore. It is interesting to note the importance the poet attached to punctuation; in each version of the poem before it was finally included in *Verses*, there are variations in the use of commas, semicolons, and exclamation points. In the revision for *Verses*, he decided in three instances in favor of colons, a mark which appears frequently in his verse.

8. AMOR PROFANUS

First printed as Number 8 in *Verses*. Only the evidence in the poem itself can account for the surmise that this was one of the poems which Dowson wrote quite late, possibly while he was collecting his earlier poems for the volume *Verses*. The love theme most recurrent in Dowson—that in "Amor Umbratilis" and "You would have understood me had you waited," love retiring and unrequited—takes a different turn in this poem. The shadows and pallid lips are still here, but the supplication to Lalage is to seize the moment, to "pluck the pretty, fleeting flowers." The Herrick-like note, however, is well submerged in the somber tone of the poem.

Gabriel de Lautrec, to whom the poem was inscribed, was one of Dowson's more intimate acquaintances in Paris from 1895. He was exactly the same age as Dowson and had already written some of the pieces which appeared in *Poèmes en prose* (1898). Like Henry Davray, Lautrec was much interested in English literature. Later he was to translate Havelock Ellis (*Le monde des rêves*, 1912) and Arthur Ransome's *Oscar Wilde*, (1912). Dowson regarded him highly enough to send him one of his few author's copies of *Verses*. Lautrec had written an article on the *Savoy* in the *Courier Français* in which Dowson's contributions to the English magazine were commended. (*Longaker*, pp. 198, 277, 279.)

9. VILLANELLE OF MARGUERITES

First printed in *Temple Bar*, May, 1894, under the title "Of Marguerites," and included as Number 9 in *Verses*. Dowson was especially fond of villanelles, a French metrical form having generally five tercets and a quatrain, the rhyme scheme being *aba aba aba aba aba abaa*, with the first line recurring as the sixth, the twelfth, and the eighteenth. The rigid pattern of the form evidently was a challenge to the poet, which he met with notable success. He often stated his feeling that his poems were largely for the ear: "Verses making for mere sound, and music, with just a suggestion of sense, or hardly that. . . ." (Letter to Arthur Moore in *Flower*, p. xxii). (See also "Villanelle of Sunset," "Villanelle of His Lady's Treasures," "Villanelle of the Poet's Road," and "Villanelle of Acheron.")

It has been suggested that Miss Eugénie Magnus, to whom the poem was inscribed, was one of the admirers of Dowson's verse at the time that he was in danger of becoming what Plarr called "a fashionable poet." In connection with the production of his play *The Pierrot of the Minute* in 1892 the poet was concerned about "enforced company with terrible South Kensington young ladies and fashionable Chelsea mesdames." (*Longaker*, p. 135.) By 1896, when he compiled the list of names for his dedications, his female acquaintanceship was fairly wide and varied. Although "the fashionable Chelsea mesdames" with whom he associated over the production of his play were probably well removed from his circle of acquaintances by 1896, they had at least their faint counterparts in the ladies who attended the *salons* that Davray occasionally took him to in Paris in 1895, at one of which Dowson was prevailed upon to read some of his verse. Conjecture invites the possible identification of Miss Eugénie Magnus with someone met at such an event.

10. YVONNE OF BRITTANY

First printed as Number 10 in *Verses*. It is one of the many poems in which Dowson celebrates the beauty of innocence, and one of several in which a stylized setting in Brittany appears. (See "In a Breton Cemetery" and "Breton Afternoon" in *Decorations: In Verse and Prose*, and the prose tale "Apple Blossom in Brittany," which appeared in the *Yellow Book*, October, 1894.) Of the poet's fondness for Brittany, Edgar Jepson wrote: "I think he was happiest in the remote Breton villages whither he now and again withdrew himself, and from which he wrote his most delightful letters. They used to give me the impression that the world went well with him there—as well, at any rate, as it could ever go with him" ("The Real Ernest Dowson," *The Academy*, November, 1907). In a letter to Henry Davray written from Pont-Aven sometime in the spring of 1896, Dowson said: "I wish you could come too and leave your fogs and bask in baking sunshine as I did this afternoon, taking my coffee in a garden of my hotel at Quimperle. I feel I shall do much work here: it is an adorable place and, much as I love Paris, where I have lived now for some time, I felt rested and restored to some prospect of reasonable health directly I came here." (*Longaker*, p. 199.)

Marmaduke Langdale, to whom the poem was inscribed, was one of the Bensonian actors with whom Dowson was intimate as early as 1891. He often accompanied him to "Poland," the restaurant over which Adelaide's father presided and remained a faithful friend to the end. He was one of the few early friends who attended the poet's funeral. His talent as an actor and as a writer of verse was not notable.

11. BENEDICTIO DOMINI

Appeared originally as Number 11 in *Verses*, although it was written before November, 1893. It was one of the poems which Dowson submitted for the second *Book of the Rhymers' Club* (1894), but it was not selected by the judges, probably at the poet's suggestion. He evidently did not care much for the poem, for in a letter to Plarr, written in November, 1893, he asked: "Do you like the enclosed verses enough to include them in the Book in lieu of 'Benedictio Domini'? [Lionel] Johnson to whom I conveyed the weighty packet seems to like them best of my budget." (*Longaker*, p. 104.) Michael Holland, who owned the original letter to Plarr, copied it for the present editor, including "the enclosed verses." They were the poem "Extreme Unction," which the judges selected instead of "Benedictio Domini." It is doubtless a finer poem.

The poem was dedicated to Selwyn Image, for a time coeditor with Herbert Horne of the *Century Guild Hobby*

Horse, the periodical which printed several of Dowson's poems. Image—later Professor Image—was well known in the nineties for his erudition and taste. For a time, he kept a studio in the Fitzroy Settlement art colony, which Plarr called "a movement, an influence, a glory." (*Plarr*, p. 68.)

12. GROWTH

First printed in the second *Book of the Rhymers' Club* (1894) and included as Number 12 in *Verses*. This poem can be readily identified with the poet's attachment for Adelaide, for it was written apparently when he was most deeply in love. It is a rendering in verse of the sentiment he expressed in a letter to Plarr, written sometime in the fall of 1894: "*Die Kleine* instead of changing, altering, repelling, as I feared/hoped might happen, in the nature of things, seems to grow in grace and favour daily. What a terrible, lamentable thing growth is! It 'makes me mad' to think that in a year or two at the most, the most perfect exquisite relation I ever succeeded in making must naturally end. Yes, it makes me mad. One ought to be able to cease caring for anyone exactly when one wishes; it's too difficult: or one ought to be able to live directly in the present. . . ." (Longaker, *The Stories of Ernest Dowson*, N.Y., 1960, p. 157.) In the second stanza Dowson has succeeded temporarily in rationalizing the feeling that "the ancient good of her dear childhood" may evolve into something even lovelier. A careful reading of his work, however—poems, prose tales, and letters—indicates that this feeling was without conviction. See the prose tale, "Apple Blossom in Brittany," *Yellow Book*, October, 1894.

13. AD MANUS PUELLAE

First printed as Number 13 in *Verses*. Dowson had submitted the poem for inclusion in the second *Book of the Rhymers' Club* (1894), but it was rejected by the judges for what they considered a better poem. Dowson, however, thought otherwise. In a letter to Plarr in April, 1894, he complained: "They have chucked my Lady's Hands, and my 'Terre Promise' in favour of two verses which I like less. Mine will be a very poor show." (*Longaker*, p. 105). There are interesting parallels between this poem and Verlaine's "Mains" in *Parallèlement*. Above a MS version of the poem sent in a letter to John Lane in February, 1893 are Verlaine's lines from Number 6 in *Sagesse*:

> Rêves bénis, mains consacrées,
> O ces mains, ses mains vénérées!

Another MS version of the poem has recently come to light appended to a letter from Dowson to John Gray (see p. 173 *infra*). The undated letter was written from Bridge Dock and signed Kit Dowson, a nickname rarely used by either Dowson or his friends. The poem, with two slight corrections penciled between the lines, was introduced with an apology for "appending my muse's latest offspring."

The poem was dedicated to Leonard Smithers, Dowson's publisher for *Verses, The Pierrot of the Minute,* and *Decorations: In Verse and Prose*; and for whom he translated many works, chiefly erotica, from the French. Smithers was the publisher of the *Savoy*, without whom it is possible the magazine could not have existed. Dowson contributed poems and prose tales to the magazine during its brief but brilliant life. Opinions vary concerning Smithers' influence on Dowson. Among others, Yeats denounced Smithers and called him "a scandalous person" (*The Autobiography of William Butler Yeats*, N.Y., 1958, p. 219), but it can readily be demonstrated that the publisher was hardly the instrument of Dowson's decline. When the House of Smithers became a sinking ship, Dowson remained loyal to his publisher, and he often expressed his regard for him. Late in February, 1896, he wrote from Paris to his friend Smith: "Smithers is, all round, the best fellow I know, and it is astonishing to me how many people fail to see this, or seeing it temporarily (instance Conder, Rothenstein *inter alios*) succeed in quarreling with him." (*Longaker*, p. 171.) In an undated letter to John Gray from Paris, in connection with his decision to let Smithers publish his poems instead of Lane, he wrote: ". . . besides offering me most magnificent terms, he is one of my most intimate friends. . . ." (A.L.S., Item 126, Catalogue One, Anthony d'Offay.) Scandalous person or not, Smithers played a significant part in giving direction to, and providing receptacles for, the decadent current of the nineties. On this, see R. A. Walker, *Letters of Aubrey Beardsley to Leonard Smithers*, London, 1937; Vincent O'Sullivan, *Aspects of Wilde*, N.Y., 1936; and *Longaker*, p. 233.

14. FLOS LUNAE

First printed in the *Century Guild Hobby Horse*, October, 1891, under the title "Fleur de la Lune," along with "The Carmelite Nuns of the Perpetual Adoration" and "Amor Umbratilis"; the three poems were grouped under the title "In Praise of Solitude." Included as Number 14 in *Verses*. Yvanhoé Rambosson, to whom the poem is inscribed, was one of the poet's acquaintances in Paris during the winter and spring of 1895–1896, to whom Dowson refers in undated letters to Henry Davray: "Commend me to our friends, Rambosson. . . ." and later, "Commend me to Rambosson and all our connaissance." (*Longaker*, pp. 277, 279.)

15. NON SUM QUALIS ERAM BONAE SUB REGNO CYNARAE

Appeared first in the *Century Guild Hobby Horse*, April, 1891; included in the second *Book of the Rhymers' Club* (1894), and as Number 15 in *Verses*. Dowson himself considered the poem one of his best. Six years after the poem was first printed he recited it to Frank Harris, calling it the climax of his poetic talents. (Harris, "The Swan Song of Youth: Ernest Dowson," *Pearson's Magazine*, March, 1917.) At the start, Dowson was anxious about the reception of the poem. In a letter to Sam Smith, written in March, 1891, he expressed his concern: "I have just seen the proofs of my poem for the April *Hobby*. It looks less indecent in print, but I am still nervous. I read it, or rather Lionel [Johnson] did for me at the last Rhymers. . . ." (*Longaker*, p. 81.)

The title comes from the first ode of the Fourth Book of Horace. "Horace suggested, but Propertius inspired." (*Plarr*, p. 57.) Adopting the license of the fiction writer, Miss Marion Plarr, daughter of Dowson's friend and biographer, in her novel *Cynara* (1933) has a sensible statement concerning Cynara's identity. She has her father exclaim:

"Why, my dear Ernest, the fellow must have had a head of cast-iron to be conscious of remorse at that stage of the proceedings."

"It's not meant to be taken quite so literally," said Dowson.

"It's sensational," continued Plarr. "It's the absolute anthem of the morning after the night before. The grey willies in an atmosphere of rose leaves and Falernian. Who's Cynara, by the way?"

"She's in Horace. Book Four of the Odes."

"No, really, I mean."

"She isn't anybody."

T. B. Mosher suggested that "Cynara was Innocence and Innocence was Adelaide." (*The Poems of Ernest Dowson*, ed. Mosher, 1902.) To which a friend of Dowson's, probably Sam Smith, who knew the Dowson-Adelaide history well, exclaimed: "The incongruity of it! One has merely to glance at the poem to ask oneself what a child of twelve, whom the poet had known for hardly more than a year, could be doing *dans cette galère*." (John Gawsworth, "The Dowson Legend," *Transactions of the Royal Society of Literature*, March 24, 1939, p. 98.) In the light of all the interpretations of the poem thus far advanced—and there are many—no satisfactory conclusion can be drawn concerning its genesis. (Mark

Longaker, "Cynara," *The Explicator*, May, 1951.)
Whether Cynara was Adelaide Foltinowicz, to whom he
dedicated the poems in *Verses*, or his neglected art, or his
recurrent image for the sanctifying grace of innocence,
or a combination of all of them, makes no essential
difference in evaluating the poem as a poem—it remains
great. Holbrook Jackson and Arthur Symons, among
many others, have spoken of its excellence. It is a poem
"in which he has epitomized himself and his whole life,
a lyric which is certainly one of the greatest poems of our
time . . . he has at once said everything, and he has
said it to an intoxicating and perhaps immortal music."
(*Symons*, p. xxviii.)

16. VANITAS

Appeared originally in the first *Book of the Rhymers'
Club* (1892) and included as Number 16 in *Verses*. The
metrical pattern of the first four lines in each of the
five-line stanzas is strongly reminiscent of Swinburne's
"Garden of Proserpine"; the fifth line is an interesting
variation from the Swinburne pattern. At Oxford,
Swinburne was Dowson's favorite poet. "Dolores" he
considered one of the finest poems in the language.
Thomas reported that it was at Dowson's urgent request
that he first read Swinburne. "The Suggestion Book of
the Queen's Library still contains a request in my hand-
writing for *Swinburne's Works*. The suggestion dates
from that first year of Dowson, and was his own idea. I
remember his copy of *Hertha* and *Dolores* heavily
scored." (W. R. Thomas, "Ernest Dowson at Oxford,"

The Nineteenth Century, April, 1928.) The theme and tone of the poem suggest Number 20 in *Verses*, "You would have understood me had you waited."

Vincent O'Sullivan, to whom the poem was inscribed, was one of the poet's friends from 1896 on. Dowson's letters to Davray, written from Pont-Aven in the spring of 1896 are full of his expressions of regard for O'Sullivan and indicate the closeness of their association. (*Longaker*, pp. 277–279.) O'Sullivan was a versatile writer, a contributor to the *Savoy*, referred to by Holbrook Jackson in *The Eighteen Nineties* as a "modern of the moderns," and now recalled chiefly for his *Aspects of Wilde* (1936).

17. EXILE

First printed as Number 17 in *Verses*. Conal O'Riordan, to whom the poem was dedicated, had a MS version, sent to him in a letter before *Verses* was issued, in which there are a few variations in the punctuation.

O'Riordan and Dowson had taken a long walking trip together in Brittany and Flanders in the autumn of 1895. Although they admired one another, there were many matters on which they disagreed. O'Riordan could not understand his friend's attachment to Adelaide, and told him so. Nor was he sympathetic toward Dowson's bohemianism. "I'm afraid that Ernest . . . was completely captivated by la vie de Bohème. He saw only the picturesqueness, though I never heard him give it that name, and was blind to the squalor. But I must confess that I have a priggish and bourgeois shrinking from much that is called Bohemian." (*Longaker*, pp. 187–189.) A reading of O'Riordan's novel, *A Fool and His Heart* (1896), dedicated to Dowson, and in some measure biographical, illuminates much of the poet's attitude toward art and life. When Dowson wanted his friend to join him in Brittany in the fall of 1896, O'Riordan found such a plan inconvenient. Dowson considered his friend's refusal a desertion. "Exile" can be read in the light of these circumstances. Until 1920, O'Riordan wrote novels under the name Norreys Conell. His historical novels written under his own name, such as *Yet Do Not Grieve*, are of the first order. For a time after 1909 he was the director of the Abbey Theatre, Dublin.

18. SPLEEN

First printed as Number 18 in *Verses*. See Number 3 of the "After Paul Verlaine" poems in *Decorations: In Verse and Prose* (1899), in which the poet again uses the title "Spleen." See also Baudelaire's Number 80 in *Les fleurs du mal* and Verlaine's "Spleen" in "Aquarelles." Dowson is using the word in its Gallic sense of "without desire, satiety," rather than in its English sense. This quality of spleen, or ennui, is one of the recurrent characteristics not only in Dowson's verse, but also in late nineteenth century decadent poetry. It is interesting to compare Arthur Symons' poem "Satiety" with Dowson's poem.

Arthur Symons, to whom the poem was dedicated, was editor of the *Savoy*, an active member of the Rhymers' Club, and familiar with the French poets and artists of his generation. He wrote an essay on Dowson entitled

"A Literary Causerie" for the August, 1896, issue of the *Savoy*, and wrote a memoir of the poet in his edition of Dowson's poems, which appeared in 1905. He knew Dowson fairly well in spite of the fact that they moved in different circles and represented different attitudes toward almost everything except poetry. They had no particular fondness for each other. In one of his less refined moments, Dowson, in speaking about Symons' alarms over the possible prosecution of the *Savoy* staff for circulating what the authorities might consider licentious materials called him "a silly bugger." (*Longaker*, p. 195.) Symons' edition of Dowson's poems no doubt did the poet a considerable service; but the *Savoy* essay must have distressed the poet, and in it he did much to start a Dowson legend which has been difficult to correct. Symons, although a poet of some stature, is now read chiefly for his criticism. His *Symbolist Movement in Literature* (1899) has become virtually a classic.

19. O MORS! QUAM AMARA EST MEMORIA TUA HOMINI PACEM HABENTI IN SUBSTANTIIS SUIS

Appeared originally in the first *Book of the Rhymers' Club* (1892) and included as Number 19 in *Verses*. The long title from the Vulgate, Ecclesiasticus 41:1, is not the most felicitous indication of the theme and mood of the poem, which was highly regarded by the leading members of the Rhymers' Club, before whom Dowson read the poem in the winter of 1891. Yeats named this poem, along with the "Villanelle of Sunset," as the reason why he felt that some of the poems of the Rhymers should be given the permanency of a bound volume. (*The Autobiography of William Butler Yeats: The Trembling of the Veil*, New York, 1958, p. 200.) Symons also considered the poem one of Dowson's finest. "In this poem . . . surely the music of silence speaks, if it has ever spoken. The words seem to tremble back into the silence which their whisper has interrupted, but not before they have created for us a mood, such a mood as the "Venetian Pastoral" of Giorgione renders in painting. Languid, half articulate, coming from the heart of a drowsy sorrow very conscious of itself, because it sees its own face looking mournfully back out of the water, the song seems to have been made by some fastidious amateur of grief, and it has all the sighs and tremors of the mood, wrought into a faultless strain of music." (*Symons*, p. xxvi.)

20. YOU WOULD HAVE UNDERSTOOD ME HAD YOU WAITED

First appeared in the second *Book of the Rhymers' Club* (1894), and included as Number 20 in *Verses*. The lines in Verlaine's "Réversibilités" in *Parallèlement* have slightly different punctuation and capitalization, and *ses* in the original yields to *ces* in Dowson's epigraph.

> O les vagues Angélus!
> (Qui viennent d'où?)
> Vois s'allumer les Saluts
> Du fond d'un trou.
> Ah, dans ses mornes séjours
> Les Jamais sont les Toujours!

Ces instead of *ses* does not affect the meaning appreciably, and its use may be an indication that Dowson retained the lines more by ear than sight. The date of its appearance and its probable date of composition, "Sept. 13th. 1891" (*Flower*, p. 256) argue convincingly against the interpretation of the poem as Dowson's lament at the marriage of Adelaide to Auguste, which took place in September, 1897. The identification of "as well as he" would under any circumstances be absurd—the poet equating his love with that of a waiter in a Soho restaurant. It is enough to observe that Dowson, like many another poet, found unrequited love a theme and mood recurrently compulsive.

21. APRIL LOVE

First printed as Number 21 in *Verses*, the poem shows a serene resignation unusual with Dowson. If it is true that he was the sort of man who, instead of expecting too much from life and love, expected too little—"less even than was there," as he has his character Philip Rainham say in *A Comedy of Masks*—the poem can be read as a reflection of what he called "an immense lassitude, born neither of satiety nor of disappointment."

Arthur Cecil Hillier, to whom the poem was inscribed, was a member of the Rhymers' Club with whom Dowson took a walking trip in Brittany in the summer of 1890. It was Hillier, along with G. A. Greene, the secretary of the Rhymers' Club, who collaborated with Dowson on the translation of Richard Muther's *Geschichte der Malerei im neunzehnten Jahrhundert*, which was issued

NOTES

in three volumes totaling 2,304 pages in 1895–1896. Dowson, whose German was slight, did little of the actual translating; his work was largely restyling the relatively literal translations of Hillier and Greene.

22 and 23. VAIN HOPE and VAIN RESOLVES

First printed as Number 22 and Number 23 in *Verses*, these two poems may well be considered together, for they are not only companion pieces in sentiment, but they both employ a direct-discourse monologue pattern, with a long ten-syllable line. The second of these poems was written as early as December 3, 1891 (*Flower*, p. 257), and it is reasonable to assume that "Vain Hope" was written at virtually the same time. Were it not for the evidence of time of writing, these poems, especially stanzas 2 and 3 of "Vain Resolves," might readily be assigned to a period later than the time of the dedicatory epistle to Adelaide.

24. A REQUIEM

First printed as Number 24 in *Verses*. Dowson probably drew Neobule, to whom the poem is addressed, from Horace, Book III, 12, rather than from the Greek Neobule, who, according to tradition, was the beautiful girl who was promised and then refused as the bride of the poet of Paros, Archilochus. The parallels, however, between the Greek Neobule and the figure addressed in Dowson's poem are interesting, and invite pursuit. Horace's "Ad Neobulen" and the Persephone legend are the most likely sources for the name and the particular connotations in this poem. In this connection, Arthur Symons observed: "He used the commonplaces of poetry frankly, making them his own by his belief in them: the Horatian Cynara or Neobule was still the natural symbol for him when he wished to be most personal. (*Symons*, p. xxv.)

John Gray, later Canon Gray, to whom the poem was dedicated, was the author of a collection of delicately wrought verse entitled *Silverpoints* (1893) which Dowson greatly admired and which influenced him in the writing of his prose tales in *Dilemmas* (1895). Of Gray he wrote to Plarr: ". . . this morning Gray who is finally leaving the Temple—quantum mutatus ab isto—fat but friendly, I fear incurably given over to social things—and about to take up his abode in Park Lane! This is sad." (*Plarr*, p. 72.) Gray was a Roman Catholic from youth, but there is no indication that he was an influence on Dowson's conversion.

25. BEATA SOLITUDO

First printed as Number 25 in *Verses*. The title Dowson had used in English "In Praise of Solitude" for a series of three poems which were printed in the *Century Guild Hobby Horse*, October, 1891. (See note to "Amor Umbratilis", above.)

Sam Smith was an acquaintance of Dowson's at Oxford. Later, in London, he was probably the poet's most intimate friend, for it was to Smith that he wrote most fully about his love affair with Adelaide. John

Gawsworth has arranged these letters in a sequence which affords an illuminating—and painful—record of the growth and decline of the Dowson-Adelaide relationship. ("The Dowson Legend," *Transactions of the Royal Society of Literature*, March 24, 1939.)

26. TERRE PROMISE

Printed for the first time as Number 26 in *Verses*, but the poem with a few slight differences was in circulation in manuscript before the second *Book of the Rhymers' Club* (1894) was issued. It was either rejected by the judges or else Dowson withdrew it for inclusion in the second anthology. In an undated letter to Plarr, he wrote: "They have chucked my Lady's Hands, and my *Terre Promise* in favour of two verses which I like less. Mine will be a very poor show." (*Longaker*, p. 105.) In an undated letter to G. A. Greene, secretary of the Club, there is an indication that the poet withdrew it before the judges had made their selection. (*Flower*, p. 258.) Although the poem is hardly as good as those which were selected for the Rhymers' collection, it is understandable why the author should like it. Its theme is in keeping with the dedication to Adelaide.

Herbert Horne, to whom the poem was inscribed, was coeditor of the *Century Guild Hobby Horse*, in which several of Dowson's early poems were printed. Edgar Jepson considered Horne's periodical the link between the Pre-Raphaelites and the poets of the nineties. (*Memories of a Victorian*, London, 1933, Vol. I, p. 102.) Dowson's letters show a high regard for Horne as a man and an editor. For Horne's part in the Rhymers' Club, see *Plarr*, p. 63.

27. AUTUMNAL

First printed as Number 27 in *Verses*. Three of the four stanzas of the poem were in circulation as early as October, 1892, for in a letter to Plarr written at that time Dowson said: "My muse awoke from her torpor of many months yesterday: here is her feeble utterance, but she may run to another verse by & by." Then follow the three stanzas entitled "In Autumn," to which he added a stanza for its printing in *Verses* under the title "Autumnal." The added stanza beginning "Beyond the pearled horizons lie," although not unfortunate in its construction and sustaining of the theme, is really gratuitous. The differences in the three-stanza MS version and the text of the poem in *Verses* are largely in punctuation. (*Plarr*, p. 62.)

Alexander Teixeira de Mattos, to whom the poem was inscribed, was the managing editor of the Lutetian Society, which undertook the translation of Emile Zola's novels into English at a time when Zola was under a rigorous ban in England. Writing as scholars and protected by prohibitive prices, the translators felt secure against prosecution. After some disagreement with the editor and George Moore, Dowson was assigned *La Terre*. Teixeira himself translated *Pot-Bouille*. Dowson liked neither his assignment nor the editor, although by 1896, when he was considering names for his dedications, he had forgotten most of the difficulties which attended the translator-editor relationship. (*Longaker*, p. 131.)

28. IN TEMPORE SENECTUTIS

First printed as Number 28 in *Verses*. It was written sometime before October 24, 1892, however, for in a letter to Plarr written at that time, Dowson appended the poem virtually as it stands in *Verses*. A motto drawn from the Vulgate, *Junior fui etenim senui* (Psalms, 37:25), appeared under the title in the poem sent to Plarr. (*Plarr*, p. 69.) In spite of the difference in pronouns, the parallel between this poem and Yeats's "When You Are Old" is inescapable.

29. VILLANELLE OF HIS LADY'S TREASURES

First printed in *Temple Bar*, August, 1893, under the title "Of His Lady's Treasures," and included with slight changes as Number 29 in *Verses*. In keeping with the spirit of the villanelle, a verse form of which he was very fond, the tone here is dainty and light, without the note of somberness that is recurrent in his verse.

30. GRAY NIGHTS

First printed as Number 30 in *Verses*. This is one of Dowson's less successful achievements in the sonnet form, which he generally handled very well. In a letter to John Gray recently brought to light, the poet wrote out the sonnet on the verso under the title "To His Lady: A Nocturne." He begged forgiveness of Gray for sending him the poem, which he said had been written "after consuming many whiskeys." The repeated use of "sadlier" might seem to indicate that the poem was written in an early period when he enjoyed the effects of stylistic mannerisms. Charles Sayle, to whom the sonnet is inscribed, according to report wrote a sonnet to Dowson, one of the few verse tributes paid him during his lifetime. Sayle was a dilettante in literature whom Dowson met at Oxford, and who in 1888 introduced him to Victor Plarr, who became one of the poet's best friends and his biographer. Plarr called Sayle "the great introducer"; and it was through Sayle that Dowson obtained strong letters of recommendation for positions as librarian at various places, none of which, however, he ever accepted, either out of a feeling of incompetence or negligence. (*Longaker*, p. 162.) Sayle became Assistant Librarian of the University at Cambridge.

31. VESPERAL

Printed for the first time as Number 31 in *Verses*. Although narrow constructions cannot readily be placed on any of Dowson's poems, for the theme of life-weariness is regularly recurrent, this poem seems to have a particular occasional quality. It was written before Hubert Crackanthorpe, to whom the poem was dedicated, took his own life by drowning in the Seine in December, 1896; otherwise one might be tempted to identify the poem with Dowson's reflections at the time he learned of his friend's death. Crackanthorpe, editor of the *Albemarle*, in which Dowson's "To One in Bedlam" was printed in August, 1892, and author of three collections of delicately written prose tales—*Wreckage* (1893), *Senti-mental Studies* (1895), and *Vignettes* (1896)—was to have become the editor of a revived *Savoy*, which had expired in the fall of 1896. On October 30, Crackanthorpe wrote to the publisher Grant Richards:

> I have just heard from Arthur Symons that the *Savoy* is to cease in December. Would you be disposed to consider the idea of taking it over then with me as editor? I do not know under what conditions Smithers would be willing to cede the title: but I imagine that an advantageous arrangement might easily be arrived at. . . . I believe without vanity that my name (for certain reasons which I need not specify) would be more valuable than Symons', and certainly yours would be an improvement on that of Smithers . . . we should make a fresh start; break away from 'the Beardsley tradition' and have, I think, a very fair chance of success. . . . (Grant Richards, *Author Hunting*, New York, 1934, p. 18.)

Dowson, of whom both Crackanthorpe and Richards thought highly, although loyal to Smithers, looked forward to the revival of the *Savoy* and planned to contribute to it. (*Longaker*, p. 228.)

32. THE GARDEN OF SHADOW

First appeared in the second *Book of the Rhymers' Club* (1894); included as Number 32 in *Verses*, with two slight changes in the punctuation. Written before December, 1894, the poem can be interpreted rather as a statement of the poet's lack of confidence in his ideal of love for Adelaide than as a reflection on the end of his relationship with her. This is only one of the many poems in which the aftermath of love is anticipated and celebrated long before the poet abandoned hope in the realization of his ideal.

33. SOLI CANTARE PERITI ARCADES

First printed as Number 33 in *Verses*. The title is drawn from Virgil, *Eclogues* 10, 32–33, and can be translated: "Arcadians, alone gifted to sing." (Compare the brief prose poem "Markets" in *Decorations: In Verse and Prose*.) The poem is hardly representative of Dowson's usual theme and manner, which are uncongenial to the pastoral mode; in fact, it is as jocular as Dowson ever was, or could be. Aubrey Beardsley, the talented illustrator in the *Yellow Book* and the *Savoy* to whom the poem is somewhat inappropriately inscribed, provided the binding block for *Verses* and the illustrations for *The Pierrot of the Minute* (1897), which he called a "tiresome playlet." (*Plarr*, p. 66.) Mabel Beardsley, the artist's sister, played the role of the Moon Maiden in one of the early productions. Dowson admired Beardsley, and even wanted to like him; Beardsley, on the other hand, disliked the poet and made no attempt to conceal his feeling. (*Longaker*, p. 184.)

34. ON THE BIRTH OF A FRIEND'S CHILD

First printed as Number 34 in *Verses*, this is one of Dowson's few occasional poems, a kind of verse in which he had little interest or talent. The poem is obviously an attempt to state cleverly and at the same time sincerely his regard for Victor and Nellie Plarr, whose daughter Marion was born on September 2, 1893. "We were," wrote Plarr, "of course greatly touched by the lines, though one could have wished that a more Dowsonian meter had been adopted than the easily written eighteenth century couplet." (*Plarr*, p. 89.) The daughter Marion was to write a fictionalized account of Dowson and Adelaide entitled *Cynara* (London, 1933).

35. EXTREME UNCTION

Appeared in the second *Book of the Rhymers' Club* (1894) and included as Number 35 in *Verses*. Variations in capitalization and punctuation are numerous between the two texts, no one of which, however, changes the theme and manner of the poem significantly. Plarr, who received a copy of the poem on the back of a sheet in one of Dowson's undated letters, consistently entitles the poem "Supreme Unction." (*Plarr*, pp. 18, 82, 120.) It is only barely possible that Dowson had this as his original title. His biographer, writing largely from memory twenty years after he first received the poem, might have been in error. For the possible influences of Flaubert, Zola, and Pater, see Katherine Wheatley, "Ernest Dowson's 'Extreme Unction'," *Modern Language Notes,* May, 1923. The sacramental rite of extreme unction was borne vividly to Dowson's mind in the spring of 1893 during the illness and death of Joseph Foltinowicz, Adelaide's father, who was a devout Catholic. Dowson was a constant visitor at "Poland" during this time, and he attended the funeral. It was suggested by

Sam Smith, to whom the poet wrote a detailed letter about the situation at "Poland" at the time, that "Extreme Unction" grew out of the circumstances surrounding the death of Foltinowicz. Lionel Johnson, to whom the poem was dedicated, was a close friend of long standing from Dowson's Oxford days. Here the dedication was quite appropriate, for Johnson was a Roman Catholic, and he told Dowson he liked this poem better than any of the verses the poet submitted for inclusion in the second *Book of the Rhymers' Club.* An active member of the Rhymers' Club, a very good poet and critic, Johnson was to have contributed to a volume of verse by Dowson and Plarr. (*Longaker*, p. 232.) Johnson's conversion and distinctive kind of Catholicism no doubt had an influence on Dowson's entrance into the Church.

36. AMANTIUM IRAE

First printed as Number 36 in *Verses.* The title was drawn from Terence, *Andria*, Act III, Scene 2. Flower suggests a possible relationship between Dowson's "Nevermore" in line 18 and Poe's "Raven." (*Flower*, p. 262.) Verlaine's poem entitled in English "Nevermore" in *Melancholia* is, in the light of the theme and mood of the poem, an interesting parallel.

37. IMPENITENTIA ULTIMA

Appeared originally in the first issue of the *Savoy*, January, 1896. Included as Number 37 in *Verses* with a few changes in the punctuation, and "whilst" altered to "while" in line 15, and "soul" changed to "life" in line 17. There are parallels between the poem and the prose tale "The Eyes of Pride," which appeared in the same issue of the *Savoy*. Whether Symons, in reading the manuscripts of the poem and story, understood their abject sincerity cannot be determined, although by the time they were submitted he and many others were aware of the Dowson-Adelaide relationship. Robert Harborough Sherard, to whom the poem was inscribed, was one of the poet's most faithful friends. It was Sherard who found Dowson ill and destitute in mid-January, 1900, and took him to his home in Catford, where, after six weeks of apparently improving health, the poet died. Biographer and translator, Sherard was not well liked by the Symons circle, and his testimony about Dowson and others is at times discounted by those who had little opportunity to know the poet intimately. Dowson himself called Sherard "the most morose and spleenful person I have yet encountered. His conversation is undiluted vitriol." (*Plarr*, p. 72.) And yet, no one who is charitably disposed will try to discount Sherard's role of Good Samaritan. For a detailed account of Dowson's last days in Sherard's home, see *Longaker*, pp. 257–269.

38. A VALEDICTION

First printed as Number 38 in *Verses*. Written in 1893, four years before the marriage of Adelaide and Auguste, the poem with its line "If we must part" indicates that even at an early stage in the love affair, the poet had little confidence in its fulfillment. The anguished cry of

"Impenitentia Ultima" can readily be reconciled with the faint hope expressed in "A Valediction" if one takes into account the direction which the poet's attachment for Adelaide had taken.

39. SAPIENTA LUNAE

First printed as Number 39 in *Verses*. Stanzas 1 and 2, at least, with notable differences, were written as early as February, 1892, for in an undated letter to Plarr, written soon after the first *Book of the Rhymers' Club* (1892) appeared, Dowson ended:

To quote mes derniers—

> The wisdom of the world said unto me:
> "Go forth and run; the race is to the brave;
> Perchance some honour tarrieth for thee!"
> "As tarrieth," I said, "for sure the grave!"
> For I had pondered on the rune of roses,
> Which to her votaries the moon discloses.
>
> "Yea," said I, "for her eyes are pure and sweet
> As lilies, and the fragrance of her hair
> Is many laurels; and it is not meet
> To run for shadows when the prize is here."
> This said I, knowing all the rune of roses,
> Which in her hour, the pale, soft moon discloses.

Dowson's "moon wisdom" unlike Yeats's in "The Phases of the Moon" and *A Vision*, is a poetic device rather than an attempt to apply insight to his theme. I have been unable to identify André Lebey, to whom the poem was inscribed. The poet's letters written at the time the dedications were being considered are full of references to his acquaintances, but Lebey's name does not appear. A likely surmise is that he was one of the many men with whom the poet struck up a brief acquaintance in Paris in 1895–1896.

40. CEASE SMILING, DEAR! A LITTLE WHILE BE SAD

First printed as Number 40 in *Verses*. The line from Propertius, Book II, xv, 23, can be rendered: "While the fates allow us, let us satisfy our eyes with love." Plarr reported: "Ernest Dowson loved his Propertius. . . . There is a singular, a poignant parallelism between the great and prolonged *cri du coeur* of the old Roman and the modern's sorrowful lament. . . ." (*Plarr*, p. 57.) If the poem is interpreted as a reflection of a stage in the poet's love for Adelaide, it was written quite early, for here the poet is more concerned with the passing of youth and innocence than with unrequited love. Cf. "Growth," Number 12 in *Verses*.

41. SERAPHITA

First printed as Number 41 in *Verses*. Among Dowson's "Hitherto Unpublished Poems" there are some verses entitled "Seraphita-Seraphitus" (*Flower*, p. 142), which understandably the poet did not select for inclusion in *Verses* or in his later volume *Decorations*. The sonnet "Seraphita" included in *Verses*, especially the sestet, lacks Dowson's customary restraint.

42. EPIGRAM

First printed as Number 42 in *Verses*. In the section "Hitherto Unpublished Poems," Flower has included an earlier version of this poem which was originally entitled "A Requital" and dated May 29, 1894. Save for the usual differences in punctuation, and two slight changes in wording, the versions are similar, and both illustrate the poet's talent for brevity and clarity.

43. QUID NON SPEREMUS, AMANTES?

First printed as Number 43 in *Verses*. In a letter to Plarr, he appended the poem with the date April 9, 1894. The theme of the poem might indicate that the title instead of reading, "What do we hope for, lovers?" might well read "What do we lovers hope for?" The Latin title could have been drawn from any number of Roman poets, although in this instance it is possible that it is Dowson's own.

Arthur Moore, to whom the poem was dedicated, collaborated with Dowson on two published novels, *A Comedy of Masks* (1893) and *Adrian Rome* (1899). The late Mr. Moore shed considerable light on this literary partnership in his letters to the present editor. "We did very little by way of revision of each other's work, alterations being rarely more than a few words in a chapter. . . . The homogeneity of style is, perhaps, to some extent explained by the fact that we both sat at the feet of the same authors. It was, in fact, the discovery that we both were enthusiastic about the earlier work of

Henry James which first brought us together in our Oxford days." (Longaker, *The Stories of Ernest Dowson*, New York, 1960, p. 5.) An attempt to identify particular passages with each author can be made after recalling that Moore said that their plan called for writing alternate chapters, and that Dowson "batted first" in *A Comedy of Masks*. It was Moore, at Dowson's earnest request, who carried the poet's wedding present to Adelaide at the time of her marriage in late September, 1897.

44. CHANSON SANS PAROLES

First printed as Number 44, the last poem in *Verses*. The similarity of theme and mood of this poem and Verlaine's Number 1 of "Ariettes oubliées" in *Romances sans paroles* can readily be detected. As the last poem of the volume, it supports only remotely the idea advanced by W. R. Thomas and others that the poems in the volume constitute a sequence "whose unity needs emphasizing." Although there is no doubt that Dowson planned the arrangement of the poems carefully, the last poem and a number of others hardly support the idea of a well-deliberated sequence.

DECORATIONS: IN VERSE AND
PROSE (1899)

Dowson's second volume of verse was issued in the fall of 1899 by Leonard Smithers, who published virtually all of his works, including more than six translations from the French. It was a slender volume of fifty pages, square crown, 8vo, printed with Smithers' fastidious taste on handmade paper and bound in parchment. Guy Harrison, who supplied the bibliography for Victor Plarr's *Ernest Dowson* (1914), was in error in naming Aubrey Beardsley as the designer of the cover. Beardsley had been dead for some time. Althea Gyles, who was not one of the "Smithers people," made the simple design. I have been unable to determine the size of the printing, but it is reasonable to assume that it was about the size of that of *Verses*, 350 copies. The proofs for the volume, in the collection of the late J. Harlin O'Connell, the poet corrected before August 31, 1899. Dowson died on February 23, 1900, soon after the book appeared. The book was scantily, but not unfavorably, reviewed.

The title *Decorations: In Verse and Prose* was selected over the originally proposed title, *Love's Aftermath: Poems in Verse and Prose*, only a short time before the book went to press. The probable reasons for this last-minute change are that Dowson must have realized that with the exception of the introductory poem "Beyond," with its initial phrase "Love's aftermath," and the poems "Dregs" and "To a Lost Love," few of the poems in the collection were in keeping with the original title. It is also possible that the change resulted from his feeling that he had already identified his work too directly with Adelaide, and that his readers would welcome a less personal sentiment in the title.

Dowson's decision to issue a second volume was no doubt influenced by the reception which had greeted *Verses* and the encouragement his friends gave him to publish more of his poetry. Lionel Johnson and Oscar Wilde—especially the latter, with whom the poet associated frequently in 1898—told him to devote his time and talent to what Wilde called his "own work." Wilde recognized Dowson's competence as a translator; in fact, it was he who said that of all the poets, Dowson was best equipped to put Pierre Louÿs *Aphrodite* into English, but he felt that the poet was wasting his time in translating such pieces as *Les liaisons dangereuses* of Choderlos de Laclos, even were Smithers to pay him more than he did. The encouragement of his friends, including his French acquaintances Davray and Lautrec, both of whom had done much to bring Dowson's poetry to the attention of the Parisian literati, led him to start a second "Poesie Schublade" in November, 1897. This manuscript book, which he called half-heartedly "Fragments," never grew to a sizable volume as had the earlier "Schublade," and very few of the poems in *Decorations* were drawn from that source.

The unity which some of the readers thought they

detected in *Verses* is obviously lacking in the second book. *Decorations* is a miscellaneous assortment, in which verse translations of Verlaine, exercises in the villanelle, the rondeau, and polyphonic prose, and even some of his juvenilia, find a place. It was probably difficult for the poet to find enough of his past work to give sizable volume to the collection, nor was he apparently able to drive his muse into producing something which he considered worthy of inclusion. The quality of the poems is uneven, ranging from the contrived and ineffectual "Exchanges" to "A Last Word," one of his finest poems, written long before the idea of even a first volume had occurred to him. As in the earlier volume, the most frequently encountered themes are unrequited love and life-weariness. Although it must be admitted that *Decorations* is not on the consistently high level of *Verses* there is enough good poetry in the book to justify its existence and preservation.

In commenting on the quality of the verse in *Decorations*, Plarr stated: "To me, it marks an extreme falling away of the poet's powers. It is full of lassitude and sorrowfulness, as of a man who has done with the world and is dying disillusioned." (*Plarr*, p. 120.) Plarr's feeling may have been shaped in some part by his knowledge of his friend's failing health and irregular habits in the months preceding the appearance of the book. It must be borne in mind, however, that many of the poems included in *Decorations* had been written and had appeared in London magazines much earlier, in fact, some of them earlier than the time that many of the poems in *Verses* were written. "Moritura," for example, was one of the last poems in *Decorations*, but it had been printed in *London Society* as early as March, 1887. Nor is there a clear relationship between the time of composition and the quality of the verse. The prose poems which form part of the second volume, especially "The Visit," were written quite late and still they are as fine as anything in the Dowson canon.

In *Decorations*, the author forsook the practice of inscribing poems to his friends. His list had been pretty well exhausted in the earlier volume; in fact, many of those poems were without dedication. The second book stood without any dedicatory epistle.

BEYOND

First printed in *Temple Bar*, September, 1893, under the title "A Roundel." In the first manuscript book, the poem appears under the title "To Hélène a Roundeau" and is dated August, 1889. The title in the "Poesie Schublade," as well as the date, indicates clearly that the poem was written in the pre-Adelaide stage and can therefore have no bearing on the end of that love affair. I have been unable to determine who Hélène was, although it is possible that she was another of the poet's abstractions—an earlier and lesser Cynara. The position of the poem in *Decorations* and the theme, conveyed in the initial phrase and the refrains, might seem to justify the poet's original intention of calling the volume *Love's Aftermath*. A MS version of the poem, now in the possession of C. Warren Force of New York, is interesting to compare with the poem as it appears in *Decorations*.

Loves's aftermath! ywis the time is now
That we must gather in, alone, apart,
The bitterest crop of all the crops that grow,
Love's aftermath!

My sweet—my sweet erewhile, the tears that start,
Cannot put back the dial; this is, I trow,
Our harvesting! Thy kisses chill my heart,
Our lips are cold, thy saddened eyes avow
Our short, sweet love is done—we can but part,
Dumbly and sadly, reaping, as we sow,
Love's aftermath.

The poet's inspiration might have been waning in 1898,
but the revised version of the poem as it appeared in
Decorations indicates that his critical sensibilities were
severe and abiding.

In Verse

1. DE AMORE

First printed as Number 1 in *Decorations*. It is one of
the few poems which he wrote out in his second manuscript book, "Fragments," started in November, 1897.
The length and ponderous tone of the poem contrast
sharply with the customary brevity and delicacy of the
poet's manner, as does the argumentative note, as if the
poet feels obliged to justify his love-plight. The poem is
interesting, however, in that it is one of Dowson's few
attempts to put his particular kind of love into some sort
of perspective.

2. THE DEAD CHILD

First printed in *Atalanta*, February, 1893. Included, with a few minor changes in punctuation and wording, as Number 2 in *Decorations*. The death of the little daughter of the foreman at Bridge Dock during the time that Dowson was a kind of bookkeeper for his father's dry-dock was probably the situation out of which this poem grew. The occasional presence of the child romping in the gloomy office and yard of Bridge Dock helped to make Dowson's chores over the ledgers tolerable. "It was as an adorer of childhood that his lovers and friends, who have kept his memory green, will best remember him." (*Plarr*, p. 79.) I have been unable to obtain precise information about the age of the little girl at the time of her death; but she might have been at least in part the source of the poet's eight-poem sequence of sonnets "Of a Little Girl." (*Flower*, pp. 122 ff.) It is unlikely that she was the same little girl to whom the first sonnet in the series was written, with its "In Memoriam, H. C. ob. Feb. 24, 1886." In an undated letter to Charles Sayle, Dowson expressed his satisfaction over the appearance of the poem in *Atalanta*.

3. CARTHUSIANS

First printed as Number 3 in *Decorations*. Except for the concluding stanza in "Breton Afternoon," this is the only devotional poem in the volume. It was written on May 27, 1891, probably as the outcome of the poet's visit to the Carthusian foundation at Cowfold in Sussex, the impressions of which he recorded in a letter to Arthur Moore. (*Flower*, p. 267.) Compare "The Nuns of the Perpetual Adoration," Number 2 in *Verses*, a poem written at about the same time. The two poems might be considered companion pieces, with monks instead of nuns in the poem in *Decorations*.

4. THE THREE WITCHES

First printed in the *Savoy*, October, 1896, and included as Number 4 in *Decorations* with a few changes in punctuation. The simple iambic pattern with the four-line stanzas rhyming *abab* is given an interesting variation in the last stanza of three lines which repeats lines 1, 3, and 4 of stanza two in the order of 3, 1, and 4.

5. VILLANELLE OF THE POET'S ROAD

First printed as Number 5 in *Decorations*. Its Herrick-like theme of "Gather ye rosebuds while ye may" is surrounded by an opposing life-weariness theme expressed in the repeated "Yet day is over long" in lines 3, 9, 15, and 19. As Dowson's corrections on the proof indicate, he was aware of the effect that such a structural pattern created.

6. VILLANELLE OF ACHERON

First printed as Number 6 in *Decorations*. It was taken from the poet's "Poesie Schublade," in which its title was simply "Villanelle" and dated "25/3/90." (*Flower*,

p. 269.) "Acheron," the river of woe in Hades, is the keyword in both the structure and mood of the poem, appearing in lines 1, 6, 12, and 18. An interesting variation in the construction of this villanelle is not only the repetition of line 1 as lines 6, 12, and 18; but also the repetition of line 3 as lines 9, 15, and 19. By a cunning manipulation of the unrepeated lines, the poet manages to conceal the effect of auditory monotony.

7. SAINT GERMAIN-EN-LAYE
(1887–1895)

First printed in the *Savoy*, April, 1896, and included as Number 7 in *Decorations* with slight changes in punctuation. For the issue of the *Savoy* in which the poem originally appeared, Dowson submitted the prose tale "Countess Marie of the Angels" and another poem "In a Breton Cemetery." Symons took the story, but rejected the poem, or put it aside for a later issue. (*Longaker*, p. 193.) The dates which form part of the title are indicative of the changes the poet felt he had experienced within himself, with the connotations of summer and winter intensifying the contrast. A MS version of the poem was included in a letter to John Gray written from the rue St. Jacques in January, 1896.

8. AFTER PAUL VERLAINE, I

First printed as Number 8 in *Decorations*. The translation was made as early as September 8, 1891. (*Flower*, p. 270.) The Verlaine poem, untitled save for the epigraph from Rimbaud, was Number 3 of a group entitled "Ariettes Oubliées" in *Romances sans paroles* (1874), a collection of which Dowson was especially fond. In order to provide the reader with an indication of the quality of Dowson's translations from the French, I quote the original.

> Il pleut doucement sur la ville.
> (Arthur Rimbaud)

> Il pleure dans mon coeur
> Comme il pleut sur la ville,
> Quelle est cette langueur
> Qui pénètre mon coeur?

> O bruit doux de la pluie
> Par terre et sur les toits!
> Pour un coeur qui s'ennuie
> O le chant de la pluie!

> Il pleure sans raison
> Dans ce coeur s'écoeure.
> Quoi! nulle trahison?
> Ce deuil est sans raison.

> C'est bien la pire peine
> De ne savoir pourquoi,
> Sans amour et sans haine,
> Mon coeur a tant de peine.

The untranslatable *s'ennuie* in line 7 becomes "pain" in the English version; but in both spirit and letter, in metrical pattern and even in most of the punctuation, the poem is illustrative of both the feeling and the precision with which Dowson could work.

9. AFTER PAUL VERLAINE, II
"COLLOQUE SENTIMENTAL"

First printed as Number 9 in *Decorations*. There is no reason to believe that this translation was made at a time different from when "Il pleure dans mon coeur" was made, September 8, 1891. It is unlikely that Dowson had seen Verlaine at that time, but his admiration for the French poet had begun long before he heard him speak at Barnard's Inn, Holborn, on November 21, 1893; and long before he had talked with him at the Crown and the Constitutional with Herbert Horne. Although Verlaine was nearing his end before Dowson settled at the Hôtel de Medici, 214, rue St. Jacques, in the autumn of 1895, he saw him on the rare occasions when Verlaine still limped to the François Premier, which had come to be known as the "Café du Maître," and to the dingy Café Soleil d'Or. Dowson was one of the most sincere mourners at the funeral of the poet, who died early in 1896. Dowson's translation of "Colloque Sentimental," the last poem in *Fêtes galantes* (1869), preserves the meter and the direct discourse of the original.

> Dans le vieux parc solitaire et glacé,
> Deux formes ont tout à l'heure passé.
>
> Leurs yeux morts et leurs lèvres sont molles,
> Et l'on entend à peine leurs paroles.
>
> Dans le vieux parc solitaire et glacé,
> Deux spectres ont évoqué le passé.
>
> —Te souvient-il de notre extase ancienne?
> —Pourquoi voulez-vous donc qu'il m'en souvienne?

—Ton coeur bat-il toujours à mon seul nom?
Toujours vois-tu mon âme en rêve?—Non.

—Ah! les beaux jours de bonheur indicible
Où nous joignions nos bouches!—C'est possible.

—Qu'il était bleu, le ciel, et grand, l'espoir!
—L'espoir a fui, vaincu, vers le ciel noir.

Tels ils marchaient dans les avoines folles,
Et la nuit seule entendit leurs paroles.

10. AFTER PAUL VERLAINE, III
"SPLEEN"

First printed as Number 10 in *Decorations*. The translation was probably made about the same time as the others in the series. See the poem "Spleen," Number 18 in *Verses*, and the two poems entitled "Spleen" in "Hitherto Unpublished Poems." (*Flower*, pp. 135, 136.) The Verlaine original is Number 2 in "Aquarelles" in *Romances sans paroles* (1874).

Les roses étaient toutes rouges,
Et les lierres étaient tout noirs.

Chère, pour peu que tu te bouges,
Renaissent tous mes désespoirs.

Le ciel était trop bleu, trop tendre,
La mer trop verte et l'air trop doux.

Je crains toujours,—ce qu'est d'attendre!
Quelque fuite atroce de vous.

Du houx à la feuille vernie
Et du luisant buis je suis las,

Et de la campagne infinie
Et de tout, hors de vous, hélas!

11. AFTER PAUL VERLAINE, IV

First printed as Number 11 in *Decorations*. The translation was probably made at about the same time as the
others in the series. The Verlaine original is Number 4
in Section III of *Sagesse* (1881).

Le ciel est, par-dessus le toit,
    Si bleu, si calme!
Un arbre, par-dessus le toit,
    Berce sa palme.

La cloche dans le ciel qu'on voit
    Doucement tinte.
Un oiseau sur l'arbre qu'on voit
    Chante sa plainte.

Mon Dieu, mon Dieu, la vie est là,
    Simple et tranquille.
Cette paisible rumeur-là
    Vient de la ville.

—Qu'as-tu fait, ô toi que voilà
    Pleurant sans cesse,
Dis, qu'as-tu fait, toi que voilà,
    De ta jeunesse?

12. TO HIS MISTRESS

First printed as Number 12 in *Decorations*. It is impossible with the evidence at hand to date this poem, or

to identify the one to whom it is addressed. Internal evidence is a questionable source for identifications in Dowson's poems. The tone of the poem, however, would seem to indicate that it is not a "Missie" poem, and its cavalier theme and manner suggest an early date of composition. Dulcie, Essie, or Marie, brief acquaintances of Dowson's when he was just down from college, are inviting though probably unrewarding clues. (*Longaker*, pp. 143, 144.) It is interesting to note that when Dowson moved away from his usual themes, he could write with a charming grace.

13. JADIS

First printed as Number 13 in *Decorations*. It was drawn from his "Poesie Schublade" in which it is dated "August 24/89." (*Flower*, p. 271.) The title of this dainty rondeau suggests a relationship with Verlaine's *Jadis et naguère*, but Dowson's poem shows no trace of influence from the eight poems in Verlaine's collection. The poem invites comparison with "Growth," Number 12 in *Verses*, and the prose tale "Apple Blossom in Brittany" in the *Yellow Book*, October, 1894.

14. IN A BRETON CEMETERY

This poem was submitted for the April, 1896, issue of the *Savoy*, but Symons rejected it or tabled it for a future issue. Dowson then submitted the poem to the *Pageant*, where it was first printed in the Winter issue of 1897. It was then included as Number 14 in *Decorations*. The poet had been in Brittany in 1890 and again in 1892, brief sojourns which gave him background for the poem "Yvonne of Brittany," which he included in *Verses*, and for his story "Apple Blossom in Brittany" in the October, 1894, issue of the *Yellow Book*. In the spring of 1896, however, he took up residence at the Hôtel Gloanec, Pont-Aven, Finistère, which he told Plarr was to be "more or less my permanent home and address." (*Longaker*, p. 205.) In his tale, "The Dying of Francis Donne," written for the August, 1896, issue of the *Savoy*, he wrote of a Breton cemetery in the same vein as in this poem. A MS version was included in an undated letter from Pont-Aven to John Gray.

15. TO WILLIAM THEODORE PETERS ON HIS RENAISSANCE CLOAK

Printed for the first time in *Decorations* as Number 15. It was probably written as early as November, 1892, at the time that Peters produced Dowson's verse play *The Pierrot of the Minute*. Peters was an American poet and actor who came occasionally to the meetings of the Rhymers' Club and who was a charter member of the "Bingers"—the closing-time habitués of the Crown. Peters commissioned Dowson's verse play, which he directed and in which he played the role of Pierrot. He was probably responsible for the somewhat inappropriate epilogue to Dowson's delicately wrought play. (Quoted in *Flower*, p. 233.) Dowson's poem to Peters is an example of one of the few attempts he made to write occasional poetry, a genre for which he obviously did not care. The poem shows a resemblance to W. E. Henley's "Ballade of Dead Actors."

16. THE SEA-CHANGE

First printed as Number 16 in *Decorations*. It was probably written in the fall of 1896 during the poet's stay at his "more or less permanent home and address" at Pont-Aven, from which he made short excursions to the promontory Point du Pouldu, where, as the poem states "river and ocean meet in a great tempestuous frown." The poet's love for the sea expressed in line 8 is more a point of departure for the development of the theme than a literal statement. The "last great hope" in line 10 bears a faint resemblance to Tennyson's "Crossing the Bar," which Dowson liked for its music. The "one woman" in the last line can be identified with Adelaide.

17. DREGS

First printed as Number 17 in *Decorations*. The position of the poem about midway in the volume leads one to wonder why it was not placed at the end, or immediately before "A Last Word." After reading this poem with its note of finality, one scarcely expects to find it followed by "A Song" and later by "In Spring" and the blithe rondeau "Ah, Manon, say why is it we."

18. A SONG

First printed in the *Savoy*, September, 1896. Included as Number 18 in *Decorations*, with a few minor changes in punctuation. The title of the poem, justified by the refrain at the end of each stanza, is no longer the deliberately considered phrase which is characteristic of most of the titles in the earlier volume. The poems in *Decorations* which have obviously well-pondered titles were generally written before 1896. By the time Dowson was correcting the proofs for his last volume he no longer felt compelled to find decorative and ingenious titles for his poems. Generally speaking, in the matter of titles Dowson moved from the complex to the simple, with both indolence and good taste controlling the progression.

19. BRETON AFTERNOON

First printed in the *Savoy*, July, 1896. Included as Number 19 in *Decorations* with changes in punctuation, and the substitution of "land" for "world" in line 9. It was probably this poem to which Dowson referred in his letter to Smithers, written sometime in the spring of 1896: "I have done a poem in my Breton manner which I shall send you when I have worked it up a little. . . ." (*Longaker*, p. 212.)

20. VENITE DESCENDAMUS

First printed in the *Savoy*, August, 1896; included as Number 20 in *Decorations* with a few changes in punctuation. In the same issue of the *Savoy* Dowson's extraordinary study in the contemplation of death, "The Dying of Francis Donne," appeared. This minute and searching record of a man's feelings at the prospect of imminent death is a sort of amplification of the theme and mood of the poem. In the light of the circumstances surrounding the poet's life at the time these pieces were written, the poem and the prose tale cannot be dismissed as an artificially cultivated expression of the death wish or as mere rhetoric.

21. TRANSITION

Although first printed as Number 21 in *Decorations*, the poem was drawn from the "Poesie Schublade" with the date "Dec 26 '92." Flower believes that the chronological order of the poems in this part of the manuscript book supports the conclusion that there was a slip of the pen, that the date should read "Dec 26 '90." (*Flower*, p. 272.) The possible differences in the time of composition have significance insofar as the "dear child" in line 1 could be identified with Adelaide were the 1892 date to be accepted. Specific identification, however, is impossible and unnecessary to the comprehension and enjoyment of the poem, which is one of the best among the many in which he versified his statement to Plarr: "What a terrible, lamentable thing growth is!" (Longaker, *The Stories of Enest Dowson*, New York, 1960, p. 157n.)

22. EXCHANGES

First printed as Number 22 in *Decorations*. A very narrow interpretation of the poem would associate it with the few expressions of the poet's feeling that perhaps his love for Adelaide was futile because of her unworthiness.

The poem is in large measure a versification of the theme of the allegory "The Princess of Dreams" in the prose section of *Decorations*.

23. TO A LADY ASKING FOOLISH QUESTIONS

First printed as Number 23 in *Decorations*. In this poem Cynara and Neobule give way to the more conventional Chloe, apparently for the reason that the lady who asks the questions is an abstraction for a kind of love that the poet considered both confining and properly transient.

24. RONDEAU

First printed as Number 24 in *Decorations*. Although this poem is placed near the end of the poet's second and last volume, in both mood and form it would seem to be one of his earliest verses. The tone is unusual for Dowson— light, urbane, suggesting in its questioning the love poetry of the Restoration. The rondeau, a form of verse of which the poet was especially fond in his early experiments with metrical patterns, is most felicitous here. Among the almost relentless procession of poems which disclose an abject life-sickness and somberness of mood, the presence of Manon and what she represents is unusual and not unwelcome.

25. MORITURA

First printed in *London Society*, March, 1887. Included as Number 25 in *Decorations* with a few changes in punctuation and capitalization. This was one of Dowson's earliest poems to be printed, the "Sonnet of a Little Girl" preceding it in *London Society* in November, 1886. An interesting story concerning the poet's unwillingness to inform others, even members of his immediate family, about his ambitions in verse is related in one of Lewis Swan's letters to his daughter Madeleine. For a long time Alfred Dowson, the poet's father, had held in high regard a few poems signed only with initials which had appeared in a fashionable periodical. It was eventually disclosed that the author of the poems was his son Ernest. (*Longaker*, p. 63n.) The somber tone of the poem, written before Dowson was out of his teens, probably derives more from his reading early Tennyson than from any youthful compulsion to melancholy.

26. LIBERA ME

First printed as Number 26 in *Decorations*. Originally entitled "Hymn to Aphrodite," it was one of the first entries in the "Poesie Schublade," which was begun in 1886. (*Flower*, p. 274.) In the light of the fact that Dowson was only nineteen when the poem was written, such lines as "Long have I served thine altars, serve me now at the end" may be considered youthful indulgences in rhetoric. "The fierce flames" of Aphrodite's altar were to affect him in a different way from that expressed in this early poem.

27. TO A LOST LOVE

First printed as Number 27 in *Decorations*. Since the poem is entirely uninformed by any outside reference, the questionable means of internal evidence would lead one to assume that this was one of the poet's final expressions of resignation to the inevitable dissolution of his dream of Adelaide.

28. WISDOM

First printed as Number 28 in *Decorations*. The poem appears toward the end of the "Poesie Schublade" under the title of its last line: "This is the wisdom of the wise." (*Flower*, p. 274.) The changes in the punctuation and wording which Dowson made for the final version in *Decorations* are not significant. Although not so cavalier in tone as the rondeau "Ah, Manon, say why is it we" the poem is in Dowson's lighter vein.

29. IN SPRING

First printed as Number 29 in *Decorations*. Under the title "A Song for Spring Time" it appeared near the middle of the "Poesie Schublade." (*Flower*, p. 275.) On a superficial level, the poem suggests the opening lines of T. S. Eliot's *The Waste Land*, "April is the cruellest month. . . ." The metrical arrangement of the sonnet is interestingly divided into two seven-line stanzas, with the rhyme scheme *aabbcdc* and *eeffgdg* providing an unusual and pleasing tonal pattern.

30. A LAST WORD

First printed in the *Savoy*, November, 1895, under the title "Epilogue" and included as Number 30, the last poem in *Decorations*. The poem, interestingly enough in the light of its note of finality and mature retrospective judgment, was written probably as early as 1886, for it appears as Number 8 in a sequence of sonnets which Dowson entitled "Sonnets of a Little Girl," in his "Poesie Schublade." (For variations of entire lines, see *Flower*, p. 276.) Were it not for the positive date in the manuscript book, one might readily conclude that the poem was composed quite late, at least as late as the fall of 1896, when Dowson knew of the approaching end of the *Savoy* and the breaking up of the Rhymers' Club. The lines "Vain things alone/ Have driven our perverse and aimless band" have been taken as the poet's final judgment of his own art, and the art of the Decadence at large. In spite of the fact that the poem was written long before Dowson had particular cause for stating "the night is now at hand," the theme and mood of the poem are singularly appropriate to the circumstances surrounding its appearance in the next to last issue of the *Savoy*, and as the final poem in the poet's last volume.

In Prose

Since Dowson made no reference to the prose pieces in *Decorations*, and no MSS with accompanying dates have come to light, it is impossible to determine what the author's intent was in writing them or when they were written. Whereas most of the poets of the nineties were given to detailed statements of poetic theory and explanations of their own particular aesthetics—witness Symons, Yeats, and Wilde, among others—Dowson has left little save a few incidental, fragmentary comments about his theories of poetry. This, however, need not imply that his aesthetic was derivative and not thought out. To apply to him the lines of De Béranger:

> Son coeur est un luth suspendu;
> Sitôt qu'on le touche il rèsonne.

is to deny him his very considerable intelligence and to reject what must be obvious to discerning readers: namely, that he was a conscious artist who deliberated long and carefully over means for attaining particular effects. His reading in Poe's tales, especially "Eleonora," "Ligeia," and "The Fall of the House of Usher," was one of the influences which contributed to his feeling, never expressed directly but frequently implied and demonstrated, that poetry can and often does exist in prose. Many passages in the stories which he wrote for the *Savoy* and those which appeared in his collection of prose tales, *Dilemmas* (1895), bear this out. He himself preferred his prose to his verse, an extraordinary preference for one so gifted in the medium of verse. Prose, however, did not mean to him the prosaic. Properly employed, it could be a richly sensuous medium for poetry. Without any direct statement of the author's intent as supporting evidence however, the five prose pieces in *Decorations* nevertheless may be thought to represent an attempt on Dowson's part to demonstrate his well-considered feeling that poetry and prose can be a felicitous union. His familiarity with Gabriel de

Lautrec's *Poèmes en prose* (1898) may have led him to include a few prose poems in *Decorations*.

THE FORTUNATE ISLANDS

Printed for the first time in *Decorations: In Verse and Prose*. No MS versions of any of the prose pieces in *Decorations* have come to light. The proofs of both the verse and prose were in the collection of the late J. Harlin O'Connell of New York. One change is penciled in the proofs: in paragraph 2, "any dreaming" is corrected to "my dreaming." Dowson constantly sought escape from the world and from himself by changing his environment. In time he realized that a change of scene produced only temporary benefits, and that "the fortunate islands" were not man's lot. The sentiment of the piece is an amplification of two lines of verse which appear in the "Hitherto Unpublished Poems" in the Flower edition:

> In vein [sic] we cross the seas change lands,
> In search of that we know not.

MARKETS
After an Old Nursery Rhyme

First printed in *Decorations*. This trifling little piece has no counterpart in Dowson's works. The apparent naïveté of the maid is entirely foreign to the sweet innocence of the girls in all of his poems and stories. That the episode narrated has some relationship to an old nursery rhyme is the only possible justification for its inclusion in a collection which holds such poetic prose as "The Visit."

ABSINTHIA TAETRA

First printed in *Decorations*. It is a sort of "Confessions of an English Absinthe Drinker." In the light of Dowson's familiarity with the effects of absinthe the piece cannot be dismissed as only a rhetorical exercise. Frequently during the winter of 1897 Dowson must have experienced all that the prose poem records.

THE VISIT

Appeared for the first time in *Decorations*. In spite of the fact that Dowson tried to leave the impression with many of his acquaintances that his illnesses were only trifling, he himself knew how grave was the malady from which he suffered. Both of his parents were tuberculous, and his only brother, Rowland, died of consumption. Like the character in his story "The Dying of Francis Donne," his awareness of approaching death became increasingly poignant: he knew he was going to die "in a few months, in six perhaps, and certainly in a year." This knowledge stimulated and depressed him in turn. During the winter of 1898 when he, like Keats, had fears that he might cease to be, he drove himself to work until his feeble body could stand no more; and there were times, when the charcoal smoldered low and a great weariness came over him, that he looked into the countenance of the visitor who had come to him on anguished, lonely nights, and said, "I have wanted you all my life."

THE PRINCESS OF DREAMS

First printed in *Decorations*. The allegory was doubtless

written after Adelaide had spurned his love and married Auguste the waiter. According to rumor, her marriage brought her small happiness. Some of Dowson's acquaintances, out of humor with his attachment, reported that her innocence was sullied long before he lost her. But whenever he spoke of her, he defended her. In *Contemporary Portraits* (*Second Series*) Frank Harris reported a conversation he had had with Dowson soon after Adelaide's marriage. "You can find a dozen gems, incomparably more lustrous, more . . ." Harris insisted.

"More to your taste, I dare say," said Dowson, "not to mine. Can't you see that I loved her just because you and the others could find nothing in her. . . ."

This tale, however, may be interpreted by some as evidence that the poet was finally willing to believe that the tower was not of ivory and that Adelaide was neither virtuous nor a princess.

THE PIERROT OF THE MINUTE

The Pierrot of the Minute, save for the beautiful "Moon Maiden's Song" which concludes the play,[1] remained unpublished until 1897, at which time Leonard Smithers issued a small edition of three hundred copies and thirty

[1] The four stanzas of this song were printed on a four-page program which was circulated at the time of the first production of the play. Dowson evidently found the program too ornate for his taste, for in a letter to John Lane, written in December, 1892, he inquired: "Would you care to see a performance of the play described in the enclosed prospectus—the printing, and *colour* and publication of which I am not responsible for. (*Longaker*, p. 135.)

fastidiously printed and bound copies. Aubrey Beardsley
was finally persuaded, much against his will, to supply
the illustrations.[1] The play had been written in late
October and early November of 1892. In a letter to
Plarr of October 24, 1892, he wrote: "I have been fright-
fully busy, having rashly undertaken to make a little
verse play for Peters, which is to be played at Aldershot,
and afterwards at the Chelsea Town Hall: the article to
be delivered in a fortnight. So until this period of severe
mental agony be past, I can go nowhere." (*Plarr*,
p. 66.) Despite the "period of severe mental agony," he
was happy about the opportunity which Peters offered
him, not only because he needed the small income from
such a work, but also because for a long time he had liked
the drama as a literary form. While at Oxford, he gave
the impression to Thomas that the drama was one of his
chief interests (W. R. Thomas, "Ernest Dowson at
Oxford," *The Nineteenth Century*, April, 1928); and
once in London, he attended plays with considerable
regularity. He delighted in consorting with people of the
theatre. Marmaduke Langdale, Lennox Pawle, Charles
Goodhart, and many of the Bensonians, he sat with at
"Poland" and the Crown; and it was his interest in the
theatre which brought him and Peters together. The
latter evidently had the knack of getting Dowson to work
in record time, for "the little Pierrot play in verse" was

[1] While making the drawings, to which he obviously gave
considerable attention, Beardsley wrote to his friends about being
engaged with "a tiresome playlet of Ernest Dowson's." On several
occasions he referred to it as "a filthy little piece"—hardly an accurate
or charitable statement about a piece so delicately wrought.
(*Longaker*, p. 187.)

done in the two weeks allotted. In his letter to Plarr of October 24, 1892, Dowson continued: "I would this play were done: half of it is completed and I have seven days more, but the second half is mightily oppressing me." (*Plarr*, p. 67.)

When the play was turned over to Peters, Dowson's obligations to it were virtually fulfilled. Although he probably attended the first performance at the Albert Hall Theatre, there is no record of his impressions of the production, in which Peters read the lines of Pierrot and Miss Ida North played the role of the Moon Maiden. (Plarr was in error in naming Mabel Beardsley, sister of the artist, as the Moon Maiden of the initial performance. In several of the later productions, however, she did play the role.) Although he was unwilling and incompetent to assume the responsibility for many of the details of the production, he was sufficiently pleased with the play to want others whom he esteemed to see it. To a performance sometime early in 1893 he invited John Lane. "Peters has arranged to play it on Wednesday next, at 9.0 P.M. in the Studio of Miss Curtois, 5A Clareville Grove, Gloucester Rd. S.W. We should both be delighted if you could turn up there. . . . If you are unable to come, would you let me have a line by return, as on account of space, the audience is to be a limited one and I have to let the responsibilities know exactly how many people I have invited." (*Longaker*, p. 135.)

Smithers evidently had no difficulty in disposing of the small printing he issued in 1897, but it was not until Arthur Symons included the play in the first posthumous edition of the poet's works that its delicate beauty

attracted more than a limited group of readers. And when
Granville Bantock was later to give it a musical setting,
the play which had lain for four years in manuscript
without a publisher began to attain a sort of vogue. Mrs.
Rosa Newmarch, in commenting upon the work of "the
unfortunate poet" whose play inspired Bantock to such
heights, observed:

This graceful phantasy, with its setting which recalls some
exquisite scene by Fragonard, is full of suggestion to a
composer of quiet imagination, and Bantock has responded
with an almost lavish wealth of thematic material. Motive
succeeds motive as quickly as thoughts pursue each other in a
dream. . . . The work is scored for piccolo, two flutes, one
oboe, two clarinets (A and B flat), one bassoon, three horns,
two trumpets, one trombone, timpani (chromatic), tambourine,
glockenspiel, triangle, harp, and the usual strings, *divisi*.

To all of which Plarr remarked: "How would the retiring
poet, who hated the mob and dreaded any battalion that
advanced in more than twos and threes, have been
staggered by this regiment of instruments!" (*Plarr*,
p. 65.) Shortly after Smithers printed the play, Dowson
was prevailed upon to read a long passage of it before a
group at a *salon* of Madame Arnavons in Paris, at which
time Miss Maude Roudebush sang the "Moon Maiden's
Song," with music by Noël Johnson. (*Longaker*, p. 136.)
    Pressed for time as the poet was in completing the play
within the two weeks allotted him, he wrote out in very
careful longhand two copies, one for Peters and one for
Miss Ida North. I have examined thoroughly the two
manuscripts, in the possession of Mr. Lessing Rosenwald
of Philadelphia. The differences between the MSS and

the text of the play issued by Smithers are more often in the stage directions than in the lines of the play itself. For example, the MSS direction for the opening scene reads: "Enter Pierrot, carrying lilies. He stands gazing at the Temple de L'Amour." The direction following line 12 reads: "He lays his flowers before Cupid's statue; then he goes timidly up the steps to the temple." Following line 16: "A very gentle music is borne out of the Temple. Pierrot starts back—in vehement surprise." Little or no critical significance can be attached to the changes which appear in the published version. The phrasings vary, the directions are in some instances more detailed, but in virtually an equal number of instances less so. In a few instances the two MSS show differences, with the North MS usually less detailed than the Peters. This is understandable, since Peters was to be the director as well as the Pierrot. From the two MSS it is impossible to determine from which Smithers worked for the publication of the play. Bantock's notes for his musical score appear in the margins of the North MS. Dowson never referred to his receiving or working on proofs; and in 1897, with ill health and misfortune besetting him, it is possible, as Conal O'Riordan suggested to the present editor, that the differences in the stage directions in the MSS and the published play are not the result of the poet's assiduous revisions but the work of one of "the Smithers people," if not Smithers himself. It is possible that there was a third MS, from which Smithers worked, which, like many items that were once in the House of Smithers, was discarded when the publisher fell upon evil days.

In the MS copy written for Peters, there is a half-sheet attached which has no bearing on the theme of the play but which was probably intended to serve as an introductory speech to the poet's reading a passage of the play before a small group. Written in Dowson's hand, it reads:

Ladies and Gentlemen: the scene of this piece, *The Pierrot of the Minute,* is laid in the Parc du Petit Trianon on a summer evening. Pierrot chases a moonbeam in and out of the trees, a moonbeam who has just taught him to love her, laughs at him and eludes him. She says to him: "I jested not, at daybreak I must go."

From that point he probably followed the lines of the play. There is no mark in the MS to indicate the closing line of his reading.

INDEX OF FIRST LINES